2000 Questions for Grandparents:

Unlocking Your Family's Hidden History

Written by
Josiah Schmidt

SCHMIDT GEN PUBLISHING, 2014

First Printing.

ISBN 978-1-312-50098-3

Schmidt Gen Publishing
2401 16th St.
Emmetsburg, IA 50536
www.SchmidtGen.com

Distributed by Lulu Press, Inc.

For more information on family history research, contact:
Josiah Schmidt, Professional Genealogist
www.SchmidtGen.com

Table of Contents

Don't Wait!

Your relatives' minds are a treasure box waiting to be opened. Did you know that your great grandmother was actually adopted by her uncle? Were you aware that your dad was named after a former Senator who helped your family financially? Had you ever heard the story about how your grandmother almost married your high school shop teacher, but fell in love with your grandpa after he saved her little brother from drowning? You've never heard these stories, and you never will, unless you sit down and talk to your relatives.

Fantastic stories like these won't necessarily pop out in five minutes of casual chatting, of course. The person you're talking to might not have even thought about these stories in decades. The vast majority of our memories lie submerged, deep beneath our consciousness. They are not truly "forgotten". They are still there. They just need help being recalled.

You undoubtedly have things about your family you don't understand, mysteries you've never solved, facts that don't add up, ancestors you've never been able to find any information about. Rest assured, the answers are almost always out there, and they might be one conversation away. Your parents, grandparents, uncles, aunts, and cousins may be collectively storing an entire hidden history of your family in their remarkable minds. You will need some assistance to unlock that history, and that is where this book comes in.

The benefits of conducting family history interviews with your relatives do not just apply to you, the interviewer, and all of your genealogy-minded cousins. Talking to an older relative benefits the older relative too, and that in itself is a good enough reason to interview them. As they march forward through time, their friends, neighbors, and siblings begin to slip away from this life, one by one. As the world changes around them, they may feel more isolated and cut off. As their body ages and they don't have the energy they used to, it becomes increasingly difficult to get out of the house and see people. They may feel dull, burdensome, or—worst of all—forgotten.

None of these things are true about them, of course. In their accumulated years, they have become more fascinating, important, and valuable than ever before. When younger people recognize the incredible value of an older person's wisdom, experience, and treasure trove of memories, it can boost an older person's self-esteem, sharpen their mental acuity, and even help to give them a renewed physical vitality. Older people are fun, interesting, and insightful friends with a sense of humor that never fades and a perspective on life honed by decades of observation and living. They are an asset to our society in every way. When the oldest generation is appreciated, active, and healthy, our society thrives.

Unfortunately, the oldest among us won't be around forever. This book is meant to help you talk to everyone—including your children and your youngest relatives. But when you are gathering together your family's oral history, the oldest must get first priority. They are generally the ones with whom you have the least amount of time remaining.

Interviewing your relatives has many benefits. It will help you to better understand your elders. Understanding your elders means understanding decisions they've made—decisions which may have affected you. Understanding your elders means helping to prepare you for your own approaching rendezvous with old age. It helps you know what to expect in the coming years and decades. Understanding your elders means helping you to see their perspective on matters where you might not understand them or might not agree with them. Understanding your elders means helping you to understand why they are the way they are—perhaps, why they've been able to keep a cheery attitude through even the worst trials, or why they get so discouraged in other circumstances.

Interviewing also helps to form bonds with older relatives, and to strengthen existing bonds. These relatives may be gone before you know it, and you don't want there to be any regrets about time lost or opportunities wasted. These people are with you, here and now. That is an amazing blessing, and we often never see what a blessing that is until they're gone. Even if you've never had that close of a relationship with this person, there is always time to start or restart a relationship, as long as they are still here with us. Seize the opportunity.

As we age, we often look back on our younger selves and shake our heads at how foolish we were back then. How many times have you ever said, "If only I knew then what I know now"? Well, interviewing your older relatives can help jumpstart that process. Talking to these individuals can impart to you a wealth of wisdom ahead of your time. The lessons that these people have learned over the course of decades are completely accessible to you, right here and now. All you have to do is stop and listen.

Do you have an inkling of interest in history, what it was like "way back when," and why people did the sorts of things they did "back in the day"? (If you've bought this book, I assume you do have such an interest.) Why not get the answer straight from the person who lived through that era? Interviewing older relatives gives us historical context to people's lives and gives us background to why they made the decisions they did.

Did your grandpa refuse to ever talk about his dad? Did your grandma's brother disappear from the censuses when he was a young boy? Have you never been able to find out what country your ancestor immigrated from? Interviewing your older relatives can help solve family mysteries, where document trails run dry. You could spend hundreds of dollars on a subscription to a genealogy website, when the answer might be as close as a chat at the kitchen table with your great aunt Edna.

When you go to the doctor and try to fill out a chart that asks you what diseases run in your family, have you ever sat there tapping the pen on the clipboard and making (un)educated guesses? Knowing what your ancestors dealt with can have major medical ramifications. You may think all your ancestors were the picture of health and just died from old age, but a family history interview might reveal that every man in your paternal line has died from stomach cancer, or that heart disease is rife on your mother's side of the family. This information can help you make changes to your lifestyle that will keep you bouncing your great grandchildren on your knee for years to come, and will help you and your doctor know what symptoms to look out for.

Of course, you are not the only one who benefits when your older relatives divulge their life stories and family histories. Your entire family for centuries and even (with the advent of digitization) millennia to come will continue to benefit. Your children and grandchildren will have a family legacy preserved forever. How much of the story of humankind has simply been lost—swallowed by the darkness of history? We can put an end to that, right here and now. It can begin with your family, and your descendants can be the first to benefit from and enjoy this legacy.

Don't wait. The importance of starting this process earlier rather than later cannot be emphasized strongly enough. There are unique pieces of history—memories—that may only be held by one person. Like a flame that has been passed from torch to torch across many miles, a mere one person may be the sole keeper of an incredible fact or memory, and it is up to you to make sure that flame doesn't go out before it can be passed on. That memory may be fading away as age takes its toll on the individual's brain, or the memory may simply vanish when the individual departs this life.

Our mortality is always encroaching—steadily moving forward. Our mortality is not always predictable, however. Anything can happen, and any particular person may be with us today and gone tomorrow. Never assume that anyone has a guaranteed amount of time left. When one person dies, an entire wealth of knowledge, wisdom, and history is gone forever. Many of the memories that an individual holds are memories that no one else has. Some of these memories are precious ones that no amount of diligent research can ever retrieve, once they're gone. The only way to preserve these memories is for us to ask the keepers to share them with us, and for us to faithfully record them, store them, and share them with the world.

Are you ready to begin?

How to Prepare for the Interview

The first step to preparing for a family history interview is to decide what kind of conversation it will be. It can be a formal interview where you designate an hour of one-on-one face time while taking notes and recording audio, or it can be an informal chat where you meet for lunch and reminisce about years gone by. Both formats have advantages and disadvantages.

If you want to really dig out the deep and epic history of your family, you will need to arrange a formal, sit-down interview. It takes time to tunnel down through the layers of niceties and small-talk to get to the core of your family tree, to discover what makes your family tick, and to see what shapes it and binds it together. If your goal, however, is just to get some fun memories of grandpa, then perhaps all you need to do is to plan to slip some questions in while you talk over a cup of coffee.

Step 1: Arrange the Setting

Whatever you decide, the next step will be the most vital one. Without this step, you will never learn anything about your family. That step is, simply, to ask the relative if you can talk to them. It is always polite to call ahead and make arrangements before dropping in on somebody, and you will definitely want to make arrangements if you intend to conduct an in-depth interview. Call them or e-mail them and ask them if you can get together and talk with them sometime. You will probably want to tell them that you'd like to pick their brain on family history, so that they can get their mind warmed up ahead of time and drum up some good memories to share with you. You and the interviewee should decide on a date, a time, and a place for the talk, and you should make it a point to be there when you say you're going to be there.

You and the interviewee will also need to agree on a setting. Typically, the best place to conduct the interview is in their home, as that is where they usually feel most at ease, and that is where they will be surrounded by all the sights, sounds, and smells that stimulate memories of all the years gone by. However, if the interviewee has a lot of activity going on at their home (perhaps there is construction occurring on the house or they have noisy children there), or if for any reason the interviewee feels uncomfortable at their home, you may want to have the interview somewhere else, where the interviewee feels comfortable and there is little distraction (perhaps at a quiet favorite café of theirs, or at your house).

It also often helps, if you are interviewing someone whom you are not exactly closely related to (maybe a step great aunt or an older cousin who is twice removed), if you also ask someone they are close with to be present during the interview. If you don't have that strong of a rapport with the interviewee yet, then having one of the interviewee's children or one of their siblings at their side during the interview may help make them feel more at ease. Furthermore, if the interviewee draws a blank during the interview, their close family member or friend may help them along. For instance, if you ask the interviewee if they remember any of their next-door neighbors from their childhood and they say, "No," the person at their side who knows them well may interject, "Well, what about that story you've told about the neighbor lady who gave you the music box?" This may prompt the interviewee to exclaim, "Oh yes, that's right!" and subsequently send them off on a rich and informative string of memories from their childhood.

In fact, if you are not very well acquainted with this older relative whom you wish to interview, it may behoove you to arrange the interview through someone closer to them. Doing so may make the interviewee more inclined to accept your request to speak with them. For instance, you might want to introduce yourself to one of their children, tell them that you are interviewing older relatives for a family history project, and ask if you can interview their parent. The child will know the parent's schedule, will have an idea of how long of an interview the parent can handle, and will be able to introduce you to the parent in a way that starts you off with more rapport with the interviewee.

What if the interviewee lives a thousand miles away? Perhaps a phone call would be the best format for the interview. The same principles apply, in this case. Arrange the phone interview in advance, make sure the interviewee can take the call at a time and place that is convenient and comfortable for them, and—if you don't know the interviewee that well—consider involving another person who is closer to the interviewee and can help lend you some rapport with the interviewee.

What about email? Email has the advantages of allowing the interviewee to answer the questions on their own time, and not necessarily all at once, minimizing the chances of mishearing something or not catching an important piece of a story, and negating the need for you to write or type out a transcript of the interviewee's answers. You could just email the interviewee a questionnaire and have the interviewee reply with an email containing their answers.

Conducting the "interview" via email, however, has the following disadvantages: the interviewee just answers the questions that you laid out in the questionnaire, and you are prevented from asking new or different questions you might think of during the interview based on information that you don't learn until the interviewee starts talking; receiving the answers in written form won't convey the full emotional depth of the interviewee's statements, and some statements may be misinterpreted (perhaps a humorous anecdote will be accidentally taken seriously, since humor and sarcasm often don't convey well in writing); sending a typed list of dozens of questions may seem daunting to the interviewee, whereas asking those questions one-at-a-time in a relaxed, sit-down setting will seem less demanding; the interviewee may continually put off answering the email questionnaire because they're too busy, but if you lock them into a face-to-face interview in a designated time frame, you will get the answers you seek right away.

After you consider the interviewee's needs and your needs, and you decide on the format for the interview, you will need to decide exactly what you want to ask them.

Step 2: Choose the Questions

When deciding which questions to ask an interviewee, particularly an elderly interviewee, you will need to be cognizant of time limitations. You will not be able to ask every question in this book in the course of one interview. You will likely not even be able to ask every question in one section of this book in the course of a single interview.

It may be helpful for you to decide on a "theme" for the interview. Perhaps this interview will focus on the interviewee's childhood, or on their military career, or on their memories of their grandparents. You can have multiple interviews, each centering on a different topic. Coming back to chat with the interviewee multiple times will help you establish a relationship with them that will make them feel more comfortable about opening up further in the future. If they are elderly, it may also be beneficial to them to make a new friend who comes by regularly to listen to their stories.

You should prepare a list of questions before you come. Borrow as heavily as you want from the hundreds of suggested questions in this book and feel free to add any further questions that you can come up with. Try to think of specific mysteries or blank spots in the family history that the interviewee might be able to solve: What ever happened to great great grandpa Conrad's sister? Why did great aunt Myrtle have a daughter with a different last name? etc. You can craft an interview path that leads to these questions.

Don't be too strict about the list of questions you have put together, however. Use your question list as a loose guide to help you along. The best interviews will take on a life of their own and begin to proceed organically from topic to topic. If the conversation starts to run dry, you can go back to your prepared questions and use them to start pumping the "memory well" and getting the stories flowing again. Forcing the interviewee to stop talking about a subject or memory they are obviously passionate about, in order to return to the subject that you want to talk about, will only serve to cut off the interviewee's train of thought, confuse them, and make them clam up.

Step 3: Find Memory Aids

Something that will help both you and the interviewee is to find memory aids to assist the interview process. Memory aids will help you come up with questions that the interviewee can answer, and memory aids will help the interviewee access memories they had forgotten about.

An example of a memory aid might include printing off a copy of a 1940 U.S. census population schedule where the interviewee and their family appear. Perhaps seeing the names of the family's next door neighbors on the census will rekindle all kinds of lost memories about life in that neighborhood. Perhaps there will be an uncle living with them in the census return, and the interviewee will suddenly remember why the uncle was living with them, and all the uncle's funny habits, and where the uncle moved to a few years later.

Another example of a memory aid that you can bring to the interview might be an old photograph. Perhaps you have a picture from 1925 of a dozen unknown faces surrounding that of your great grandmother. The interviewee may not have seen those faces in several decades, but they may be able to tell you exactly who they all are and how they are all related, and then proceed to tell you about the personalities and life stories of some of the people in the photograph that they knew the best.

Memory aids can take on many forms. Something as simple as your grandfather's unique signature on a draft registration card, a street address from a city directory where the interviewee lived as a child, or a handmade doll that you found in the attic of your great grandmother's house after she died, can open the floodgates of the interviewee's memory bank and lead you to a whole world of history and information.

Step 4: Decide How to Record the Information

The next step in the interview preparation process is to decide how to faithfully record all this vital information. Human memory is notoriously error prone, especially when one human mind is passing a memory on to another human mind. If you throw into the mix the sloppy handwriting of someone struggling to scrawl down every word that comes out of the interviewee's mouth, you have a recipe for distorted and incorrect stories or altogether missed memories.

It will help you to have multiple forms of recording happening during the interview to ensure that you get all the information recorded, and recorded faithfully.

While you should always take notes in writing as the interview is happening, writing on a notepad is not the only form of recording you will want to utilize for your interview. You will also want something more faithful, such as an audio or a video recording. You will need to ask the interviewee's permission to record them before the interview begins, however. Preferably, you should get their permission to be recorded when you first ask them to take part in the interview. It might be seen as impolite to spring it on the interviewee just as you sit down to talk that you have a recorder and you want to use it.

While future generations might love to have a video recording of grandma telling stories about her childhood, a potential downside of this is that a lot of people are camera shy. The interviewee might freeze up when they're being glared at by a big shiny lens next to a flashing red light. Then again, they might not. You will have to use your own best judgment, based on what you know about the interviewee.

An option besides video recording is audio recording. You can use an audio tape recorder to document the interview, or these days you can also buy a small digital audio recorder at very reasonable prices. Digital recorders have the advantage of storing the data in a more indestructible and more portable format. Whereas tapes might fail to record part or all of the interview, warp over time, or be lost or destroyed, if you record audio in digital format, it can be effortlessly copied and re-copied. Moreover, once a digital file is uploaded onto the Internet (either onto a personal website, or onto an Ancestry.com account, or onto an online data storage space like Dropbox.com), it becomes very unlikely to ever be totally lost.

An audio recorder, while it may not capture the valuable images and facial expressions that a video recording can provide, will at least be less distracting than a video recorder during the interview, while still providing an accurate record of the things that were said. Having some sort of recording of all the words actually uttered during the interview will not only give you something to compare the accuracy of your written notes against, it will also provide insurance. Taking both written notes and audio/video recording will ensure that if the written notes are lost, you will still have the recording, or if the recording is lost, you will still have the written notes.

You will want to make completely sure that the recorder is fully powered, either with a full charge or with brand new batteries. You may even ask the interviewee's permission to keep the recorder plugged into a wall socket for the duration of the interview, to ensure that it remains charged while you are conversing.

You will also want to test the recorder before you go to the interview location to get a feel for how close the recorder needs to be to each person at normal speaking volume. Before you go to the interview location, while you're still at home, place the recorder a reasonable distance away from you and speak about as loudly as the interviewee is going to speak in normal conversation. You absolutely do not ever want to have to remind the interviewee to "speak up for the recorder!" That would be rude, embarrassing, and distracting. Make sure that the recorder is of good enough quality and tuned to the right settings to clearly pick up regular conversation at normal volume from several feet away.

If you are interviewing a faraway relative over the phone, you should also consider recording the audio of the phone call. When recording phone calls, it's not just good manners to ask the interviewee's permission before starting to record, it's also the law. Depending on the laws of your state and your interviewee's state, it may be considered a form of illegal wiretapping to record their phone conversation without their permission.

Recording your phone interview may be as simple as conducting your interview over speakerphone, and placing an audio recorder near the speaker. If your interviewee is technologically savvy enough, you might request that both you and the interviewee record yourselves on audio, and then the interviewee can send you their recording and you can merge it with your recording to create the complete interview. If you conduct the interview over a smart phone, there are downloadable apps like Google Voice, which allow you to record phone conversations and then download the audio files onto your computer in MP3 format. You might also want to browse the Internet for a conference call service like FreeConferenceCall.com—this website is one of several sites that will give you a phone number for both parties to call into, give you the option to record the call, and after the call is finished will allow you to download an MP3 recording of the phone conversation. Paramount in any of these options is testing. Whatever you choose to utilize, test it multiple times with different devices (cell phones, landlines, etc.) to make sure that it works well and that you get a clear recording.

Step 5: Prepare a Thank-You Gift

You will build up rapport with the interviewee, make them more likely to agree to another interview, and make them likely to offer up a good word about you to other relatives you might also want to interview, if you end the interview with a tangible "thank you". The best way to do this is to come prepared with a little gift to give them at the end of the conversation. If they have sat politely with you for an hour, with an audio or video recorder running, allowing you to pick away at some of their deepest and most emotional memories, it's the least you can do. The gift need be nothing extravagant—perhaps some simple flowers, a framed copy of a rare family portrait that you discovered, or even just a nice card.

In years gone by, small gifts like this from guests to hosts were more common. It is a practice that is part of a larger culture of politeness and thoughtfulness that is sadly waning in this day and age, but it is something that elderly individuals in particular will appreciate. Going a little above and beyond what is expected of you can only help you.

How to Conduct the Interview

After you have made the preparations and arrangements for the interview, it will come time to actually conduct the interview. There are eight key points of advice to remember during the interview:

1. Make the interviewee comfortable.
2. Be a smart note-taker.
3. Be a good listener.
4. Ask the right questions.
5. Let the interviewee guide the conversation.
6. Use memory triggers.
7. Be sensitive to embarrassing questions.
8. Be aware of the interviewee's fallibility.

Point 1: Make the Interviewee Comfortable

As mentioned earlier, you will first want to make sure that the interviewee is comfortable by arranging an appropriate setting for the interview. The interviewee's home is usually the ideal setting, because that is where they will be the most relaxed and surrounded by memories, but circumstances may make another place more ideal: perhaps your home, or a quiet café, or a park. If you don't know the interviewee well personally, having a third person there who is closer to the interviewee will also help make the interviewee more comfortable.

Make the interview a reasonable length (about one hour for each interview should be long enough to enable digging into some deep memories, but not long enough that the interviewee goes hoarse). You don't want to tire out the interviewee and make them feel like talking to you is going to become a chore.

When journalists interview politicians, it's expected of the journalist to ask tough questions and hound politicians until they divulge the juiciest answers. Family history interviews are a different ballpark. Don't make the interviewee uncomfortable by asking questions that are too personal, and don't press them to talk about something they are clearly unwilling to discuss. Doing so will make the interviewee shut down, and instead of getting some of the answers you wanted, you will get none. Pay attention to verbal cues and body language by the interviewee that tell you it's time to change the subject.

Point 2: Be a Smart Note-Taker

You will not be able to write down every single word that the interviewee utters, verbatim. If you try doing that, you will find your handwriting becoming a chicken scrawl that will be illegible when you go back later to read what you've written. Rather, you will want to write down key words that can keep your mind tethered to the stories you've heard. You will want to use short hand, sensible abbreviations, and focus more attention on writing down key information.

The best words to write down when writing short hand are the subject, verb, and object of a statement. For instance, if someone tells you that "George then decided to move to the town of Dysart," you can simply write, "Geo. move Dysart". The subject, verb, and object can be used as "memory prompts". You would not be able to remember a whole story verbatim, but a handful of key words written down will prompt your brain to remember the rest and fill in the blanks with less important words like articles and prepositions. Thus, by compressing a story into short hand, you capture the meaning of what the interviewee is saying, and can unfold the story again later.

The interviewee may tell a story about a soldier who comes home from World War 1. He wants to surprise his parents, but a family friend witnesses him getting off at the train station. She phones home to his parents and tells them that their son is on the way. When the son gets home, rather than surprising his parents, the whole family is gathered there on the front porch, waving. When writing this story, you may only be able to write down something like: "Charlie come home WW1, want surpr. Friend see & phone ahead. Fam. waving." When you are reviewing your notes after the interview, you will see all the memory prompts in that line and you will be able to fill in the blanks, fleshing the whole story back out again.

Point 3: Be a Good Listener

Being a good listener doesn't just mean being quiet while the interviewee is speaking, and not interrupting. While those are good pieces of advice, being a good listener also entails actively showing the interviewee that you are indeed paying attention.

When you're not glancing at your notepad to write your notes, make sure that you are making eye contact with the speaker. If your eyes wander around to your surroundings, the interviewee will get the impression that you have lost interest, or are not paying attention, and this will make them less enthusiastic about talking to you. Don't fidget, sigh, massage your forehead, lean the side of your head against your fist, or do anything that makes it appear you are uninterested. You may in fact be thoughtfully considering what the interviewee is saying, but you will have to actively send them that message.

Respond briefly and politely when the interviewee makes a point. Nod your head subtly and use sincere-sounding verbal affirmations (like "Mhm," "Yes," or "Wow!"). If the interviewee is telling about happy memories, smile while listening. If the interviewee is telling about a sad memory, let your face show that you empathize with them. If the interviewee tells a joke or a funny story, laugh at it.

Use the ends of the interviewee's answers as a jumping point for further questioning. This not only allows you to dig deeper into a story, it also shows the interviewee that you were listening and thinking about what the interviewee was saying. If the interviewee tells you about how their mother was a prolific quilt maker, don't just brush the statement off and immediately move on to a different topic that you are eager to talk about. Ask them about how many quilts their mother left behind when she died, or ask them if they ever got to help their mother make quilts. You never know what kinds of amazing stories these follow-up questions might segue into.

Point 4: Ask the Right Questions

The hundreds of interview questions contained in this book are intended to be a great resource for family historians talking to relatives. However, there are thousands more questions that can be asked, which are not contained in this book. Many of the questions that need to be asked are very specific to certain individuals and circumstances. You will not want to robotically go down the list of this book's suggested questions one after the other.

When you ask the interviewee how they celebrated Christmas, the interviewee may tell you: "My grandfather and I would go out on December 18th and chop down a Christmas tree, and then we'd take it home and string it with garlands." Instead of looking down at the book and responding with, "Uh-huh, now the next question is: How did you celebrate Thanksgiving?" a better next question might be something like, "What was the most fun Christmas tree trip that you and your grandpa ever went on?" That particular question won't be in this book, of course. You might not know that the interviewee had a ritual of chopping down the Christmas tree with his grandfather until after you start the interview.

You will also probably not want to ask every single question in each chapter of this book in the order that they are printed. A question in this book may be unrelated to the question printed immediately above it, and some of the questions may be inapplicable to the individual that you are interviewing (some questions are only for people with children, or people who immigrated, or people who went to high school, etc.). Use the suggested questions printed in this book as a loose guide. Feel free to cherry pick individual questions from different chapters, let this book's suggested questions inspire you to think of similar but slightly different questions, and add your own completely unique questions to put together your own interview.

You will notice that many of the questions in this book have one or more smaller, follow-up questions immediately after it. That is because getting a simple "Yes" or "No" answer is not as interesting as finding out the "how," "why," "what," "who," "when," and "where" of the story. Avoid only asking questions like "Did you ever go fishing as a child?" and leaving it at that. Follow it up with, "Where did you fish?" and "Whom did you go fishing with?" and "Tell me about the biggest fish you ever caught." If you already have a good hunch that they did go fishing as a child, save time by cutting out the "Did you fish" question entirely, and going straight for the "Where", "With whom", and "Tell me more about" questions.

Let's say that you are dying to figure out where your great granduncle was living at the enumeration of the 1940 U.S. census, because you can't find him anywhere in the census and it's driving you crazy. You might ask your grandmother point blank, "Where was your uncle living in 1940? Why can't I find him?" She might be completely unable to think of where he was living in 1940. Do you even remember the exact dates that you yourself moved from each place to place throughout your life? Probably not. However, if you get into a discussion of your grandmother's memories of her uncle, she might mention in passing that her uncle took her and her family to a water park near his home to celebrate her 10th birthday. She might have been born in 1930, meaning that that celebration took place in 1940. The only water park in the area may have been located in a certain town. When you put these pieces together, you may realize that you have just solved the mystery of where your great granduncle was living in 1940. Oftentimes, there is no direct path to the answer you seek, but the clues to the answer might be there, nonetheless.

Point 5: Let the Interviewee Guide the Conversation

This point has been made briefly, earlier in this book, but it needs to be driven home. The temptation may exist to dominate the interview and continually try steering it to topics you want to talk about, but the interviewee's richest and most vivid memories may lie in other subject areas. Be open to talking about the interviewee's fondest memories, and the topics that the interviewee is most passionate about. If the interview starts to veer away from your prepared list of questions, why not let it, and see where it takes you? You can always return to your prepared list of questions if that tangent of conversation dries up.

The interviewee may continually skip around between unrelated topics. Let them skip around. The interviewee may have recalled a rare memory for the first time in many years and feel the need to get it out before they lose it again. Let them get it out.

To repeat something said earlier in this book: forcing the interviewee to stop talking about a subject or memory they are obviously passionate about, in order to return to the subject that you want to talk about, will only serve to cut off the interviewee's train of thought, confuse them, and make them clam up.

Point 6: Use Memory Triggers

The idea of using physical memory aids was discussed in the last chapter. Bringing an old document, a family heirloom, or a photograph to the interview can be a great way to trigger long-forgotten memories. It can help you put names to unknown faces, or personalities to unfamiliar names. Physical memory aids can also help uncover entire stories and lines of questioning that you would have never even thought to ask about in the first place.

Most of our memories are submerged deep beneath our consciousness, and need some help being brought back out. You may ask someone what they did for fun when they were a child, and they might draw a blank. However, if you pick at their brain from different angles, you might eventually bring the memory back. If they can't immediately remember what they did for fun as a child, try asking them who their childhood best friend was. What kind of clothing did their best friend wear? What was the worst fight they ever had with their best friend? Do they remember eating ice cream with their best friend? The interviewee might suddenly remember the taste of the strawberry ice cream they and their friend ate together on the summer day when they rounded up the neighborhood kids for a kickball tournament. Or the interviewee might think of the flannel jacket their friend always wore, and find themselves able to still smell that tobacco scent on their friend's jacket because their friend's dad smoked cigars—the interviewee might imagine that tobacco smell and suddenly remember sitting with their friend and illustrating their own comic books when they were eleven years old.

Little sensory experiences can be strongly associated with deep-seated memories, and experiencing a sound or smell or taste from a long time ago can bring back all the people, places, and things that went with it. Harkening back to specific, sensory experiences can bring back whole slews of memories that the brain had tucked away and never accessed in decades. As long as it's not a particularly painful topic and as long as the interviewee doesn't seem to be totally bored by it, feel free to pick away at a question from different angles, because you may eventually hit a trigger that releases the floodgates of times past.

Point 7: Be Sensitive to Embarrassing Questions

Some of the suggested questions in this book are of a personal nature, and some of this book's questions ask the interviewee to reveal things that might reflect negatively on the interviewee. You will have to use your best discretion, based on how sensitive the interviewee is, and what you already know about the interviewee's past. Asking one person to tell about how their parents fought may result in the interviewee laughing and spilling out a dozen funny stories. Asking another person how their parents fought may bring back very painful memories that the interviewee would rather avoid.

Pay attention to the interviewee's body language as they're talking. A few signs that the interviewee is comfortable with the questioning include things like: looking you in the eye, having their whole body facing you, having an "open" body stance, appearing still and at ease, and giving genuine smiles that employ all their cheek muscles and actually push up the corners of their eyes.

A few signs that the interviewee is annoyed or not comfortable with the questioning include things like: glancing off to the side, facing their body slightly away from you, covering or guarding themselves (by crossing their arms or legs), fidgeting and employing self-touch gestures (like wringing of the hands or scratching of the head), and giving fake smiles that look more like grimaces. Use your best sense to judge when it's okay to continue a line of questioning, and to know when it's time to back off and change the subject.

It is okay to let the interviewee know at the beginning of the interview that if they're uncomfortable with any question, they can just say "Pass". It is also okay to preface a question with, "You don't have to answer this if you don't want to" or "Forgive me if this is too personal," but don't use that preface as an excuse to just ask any inappropriate question.

Try to intersperse your negative questions amongst more positive questions. If you ask, "When was the time you got in the worst trouble as a child?" followed by "What was your hardest teenage relationship breakup?" followed by "Did you ever flunk any classes?" all back to back, your interview may start to feel like an interrogation, and the interviewee may feel like you are judging them or writing a tabloid piece on them. This goes for overly personal questions too. It may be acceptable to ask questions like, "Who was your first kiss?" and "What was the most serious relationship you had before you met your spouse?"

and "What was the saddest memory of your life?", but if you ask them all in a row, the interviewee may feel too vulnerable and start to clam up. Intersperse these questions amongst positive questions that are more likely to elicit happy or neutral memories.

When you ask a negative question, like, "Do you ever remember your grandpa getting really angry?", follow it or precede it with a positive question, like, "What is your fondest memory of your grandpa?"

This is also an important piece of advice to keep in mind when asking about previous generations. People typically have fond memories of the ancestors that they knew and met. Even if a person doesn't have particularly fond memories of an ancestor, they often feel a family loyalty to that person and will fiercely guard that ancestor's reputation. Tread carefully when asking potentially embarrassing or negative questions about a person's parents, grandparents, or other relatives. Just because the embarrassing or negative question isn't in regard to the interviewee personally, the interviewee might still take offense. Make sure that the interviewee feels that you are painting a positive portrait of their family and are honoring their family legacy, not trying to dig up skeletons or air the family's dirty laundry in public. As family historians, we always want to find the truth and dispel false myths, but we also have to take tact and respectfulness as important ingredients any time we deal with a person's legacy and loved ones.

Point 8: Be Aware of the Interviewee's Fallibility

To repeat the last sentence of the last section: As family historians, we always want to find the truth and dispel false myths, but we also have to take tact and respectfulness as important ingredients any time we deal with a person's legacy and loved ones.

You will find, as you interview relatives for family history purposes, that much of the oral history that's been passed down is false or distorted. The interviewee may tell you that their grandparents were born in Ohio, but later investigation may turn up the grandparents' birth certificates in Tennessee. The interviewee may tell you that their immigrant great grandpa was a stowaway on a ship, but you might have already contacted an archive in the old country and found that the ancestor paid all of his emigration fees and is listed comfortably in the middle of the ship passenger list, indicating that the stowaway story is completely false.

The human memory is notoriously fallible, and even seemingly deviously deceptive. Sometimes the human brain creates memories that never had any basis in reality. When you interview a relative, take everything they say with a pinch of salt, and don't necessarily take every family legend as gospel truth.

There may also come times when you know that what the interviewee is saying is false. Do you correct them, or let it slide? Here, you will have to use your best judgment. Some things may not be worth the possibility of embarrassing or offending the interviewee by contradicting them.

If the interviewee says, "I'm descended from an Indian princess on my mother's side, and my mother always used to tell me that that's why I have such nice hair," it's not worth it to say, "Actually, I've done the research, and there is no American Indian blood in the family. Your mother was wrong." Just let them pass down the oral history that they received, and cheerfully express gratitude for telling the story to you. You don't have to believe everything they say, and there is virtually never a reason for you to assume that the interviewee is deliberately deceiving you rather than making an honest mistake.

However, if the interviewee says, "My great aunt on my father's side married a man with the last name of Smith," but you're pretty sure it was the interviewee's great aunt on his *mother's* side, you might want to press the interviewee and make sure: "Are you sure it wasn't your great aunt on your mother's side who married the Smith?" The interviewee might reply, "Oh yes, of course, that's right. How silly of me." In doing so, you may help avert errors in the interview transcript that could trip up family history researchers in your family decades or centuries in the future, and also help prevent that person from repeating the incorrect information to other family members.

If ever you do decide to correct an incorrect statement by an interviewee mid-interview, do it gently, respectfully, and briefly. If the interviewee shows any signs of combativeness on the subject, just apologize and move onto the next subject. You can print the correct information later. It's not worth derailing the interview over.

When it comes to ending the interview, it is better to do so a little early (even if you have many more questions you would like to ask). This will help ensure that the interviewee is not exhausted at the end of the conversation. Furthermore, it also keeps in line with the old adage, "Leave them wanting more." If you wait until the conversation grinds to an awkward, boring halt as you run out of things to talk about, you will not be able to leave on a positive note. If you end the interview after a rousing, fruitful dialogue that both you and the interviewee enjoyed, both of you will be much more likely to agree on another interview. Going home, re-reading the interviewee's answers, and mulling over the new information for several days or weeks may help you think of new questions or aspects of stories that you'd like to dig deeper into next time—questions you might not have been able to think of at the time you were interviewing.

As mentioned in the last chapter, it helps to bring along a small "thank you" gift to give to the interviewee for lending you their time and energy. Nothing extravagant, but it helps if the gift is meaningful and truly expresses your gratitude.

Just like during the interview, use good body language when you are finishing the meeting and departing. Compliment them on their hospitality and mental acuity; give them a firm handshake or a genuine hug; and thank them sincerely and clearly.

The key things to keep in mind when conducting an interview are to be thoughtful and respectful of the interviewee, to faithfully record everything the interviewee says, and to use your best creativity and ingenuity in the questioning process.

What to Do After the Interview

You've completed the interview, and you're at home with the reams of new information you've collected. Now what? The next step is to organize the information and put it to good use.

The notes you took during the interview will probably jump around from topic to topic. There might be a few facts regarding one ancestor, then some facts regarding a different ancestor, then a few more facts regarding the first ancestor. Conversations are like that—they are not perfectly organized into sections and subsections.

One of my favorite methods for organizing information from family history interviews is to create different files for each of the individuals discussed. Create one file for information relating to Great Grandpa Johnson, one file for information relating to Aunt Beulah, etc. If you do this on a computer, as I recommend you do, you could literally create a different word processing document for each person (which would soon get rather clunky—imagine trying to research the family and having to keep ten different documents open on your computer at the same time). Or, you could (as I further recommend) make one word processing document and type all the information into that same document in different sections. Type all the information on Great Grandpa Johnson, then start a new page in the same document, type all the information relating to Aunt Beulah, then start a new page.

It also helps to put all of the facts you gathered on your ancestors into some sort of computer genealogy program like an Ancestry.com tree or a Family Tree Maker file. Ancestry.com accounts, for instance, are free. It does cost money to be able to access records on their website, but there is no cost to get an account and host/display your family tree on their website. Using a program like this, you can skip around to each individual in the tree, inputting facts and attaching stories as you come across them in the interview notes. Then, when you're all done, each individual in the tree has a neatly organized file, with all the facts relating to each person on their own page.

Of course, to reiterate what was stated in the last chapter, don't necessarily take every family legend that you hear as fact. Family legends have a way of becoming more sensational as they pass from person to person, and the human brain can distort memories and create false ones. Eye-witness testimony to the history of your family is a great piece of evidence, and it should also be weighed against other primary sources of evidence. Before you go publishing a genealogical fact in a book, or putting it on the Web for other researchers to see and copy, make sure that the genealogical fact agrees with censuses, vital certificates, courthouse records, etc. If the piece of oral family history doesn't agree with some documentation, you may need to evaluate the veracity of the claim. It is possible that the oral family history is correct and there is an error in a document, and it is also possible that the original documentation is correct and the oral family history is incorrect.

Honing your genealogy skills in a professional manner will help you discern when a historical claim meets an acceptable genealogical proof standard. Books like Elizabeth Shown Mills's "Professional Genealogy: A Manual for Researchers, Writers, Editors, Lecturers, and Librarians" and the Board for Certification of Genealogists's "Genealogy Standards: Fiftieth Anniversary Edition" are great starting points for learning how to judge historical claims and come to educated conclusions.

The final step you need to take is to prepare for the next interview. Let the stories that the interviewee shared with you soak in, mull over these new facts and their implications, and think about new questions to build on and dig deeper into stories that surfaced in the last interview, or to cover areas you missed in the last interview. Keep in friendly communication with the interviewee and discuss possible dates and places for the next interview. As you build up rapport with the interviewee over the course of weeks or years, they may allow you to ask deeper and more personal questions. When you have time for another family history interview, remember: don't hesitate, just ask.

The Questions

Childhood

1. What is your very earliest memory?
2. Are you named after anyone, or do you know the reason why your parents gave you the names that they did?
3. Did anyone ever tell you which people were present at your birth? If so, whom?
4. Did you ever hear any stories about anything interesting that happened during or soon after your birth?
5. Was anything memorable (and perhaps funny) said by someone during or soon after your birth?
6. How many siblings did you have?
7. Did you ever share a room with siblings?
8. If so, how many siblings did you share a room with?
9. If you shared a room with siblings, which siblings in particular did you share a room with?
10. If you shared a room with siblings, how did you feel about doing so?
11. Did you ever have to sleep in the same bed as a sibling?
12. If so, which sibling in particular?
13. If you slept in the same bed with a sibling, how did you feel about having to do so?
14. If you had one or more older siblings, how did you get along with them?
15. If you had one or more younger siblings, how did you get along with them?
16. Which sibling were you the closest with?
17. Which sibling did you quarrel the most with?
18. How would you quarrel with your sibling(s)?
19. How often did you spend time with your cousins?
20. Who were your favorite cousins to spend time with?
21. Where was your first childhood home?
22. Did your first childhood home have electricity?
23. Did your first childhood home after indoor plumbing?

24. Did your first childhood home have a telephone?
25. Whom did your parents talk to on the phone most often?
26. What did your childhood house look like?
27. How big or small was your childhood home?
28. What rooms were there in your childhood home?
29. Do you remember any particular smells or scents from your childhood home?
30. Can you recall any familiar sounds or noises from your childhood home?
31. What kinds of sounds and smells do you remember when you first woke up in the morning?
32. Did everyone in your household speak English as their first language?
33. Were you or anyone in your family able to speak a language other than English?
34. If so, when and how did they learn that language?
35. Did you ever have any pets, as a child?
36. What were your pets' names?
37. Who got to choose those pets' names, and how were they decided?
38. How and when did your family get those pets?
39. Did you have to work to convince your parents to get the pet? If so, how did you finally convince them?
40. Did the pet(s) belong to you personally, or did the pet(s) belong to one of your siblings, or did the pet(s) belong to the whole family?
41. Who cared for the pet(s) (fed them, cleaned up after them, took them for walks, etc.)?
42. What was involved in caring for your pet(s)?
43. What kinds of games or activities did you play with your pet(s)?
44. How long did the pet(s) live?
45. How did you feel when each pet died?
46. How would you usually cool off during the summer, when you were a child?

47. How would you usually warm up during the winter, when you were a child?

48. What was your favorite meal, growing up?

49. Who cooked that meal the best?

50. What was your least favorite food, growing up?

51. What would your parents say or do if you didn't finish some of your food?

52. What were family meals like, in your household?

53. Did you all sit and eat together for every meal?

54. What kinds of topics were discussed at the family dinner table?

55. Were there any topics that were off-limits at the family dinner table?

56. If so, which topics?

57. Did your family ever grow, pickle, can, or home-make any food?

58. What kind of oven did you have in your kitchen, when you were a child?

59. Did you ever cook or help with the cooking, as a child?

60. Did your household ever have a cooking disaster, or a meal that turned out really badly one time?

61. If so, were you responsible for it?

62. What kind of refrigerator did you have in your kitchen, when you were a child?

63. What would your parents do for you when you were sick? Any special remedies?

64. What was the sickest you ever got, as a child?

65. Who was your best friend, as a child?

66. How did you and your best friend become friends?

67. What kind of things did you and your childhood best friend do together, that you didn't do with other friends?

68. What kind of games did you play as a child?

69. What was your favorite game to play?

70. Did you ever play any video games, arcade games, or carnival games as a child?

71. If so, which ones?
72. Which video, arcade, or carnival game were you the best at?
73. What was your favorite toy to play with?
74. How big was your yard?
75. What kind of trees or flowers grew on your property?
76. What kind of critters (bugs, birds, small animals, etc.) would you find on your property?
77. Did you ever catch any bugs or animals on your property and try to keep them as a pet?
78. Did you ever have your own garden as a child, or did you ever help someone else out with their garden?
79. Did you live in the city or on a farm?
80. If you lived on a farm, what kind of produce and livestock did your family raise?
81. If you lived on a farm, what kind of farm-related chores were you responsible for?
82. What was your favorite farm-related chore to do?
83. What was your least favorite farm-related chore to do?
84. If you lived on a farm, did you ever give names to any of the farm animals?
85. If your family farmed or made produce, did you sell it at a grocery store or a farmer's market perhaps?
86. If so, which market, and where was it located?
87. Did you have a favorite treat you liked to buy for yourself at the grocery store or the soda shop?
88. What was it, and how much did it cost you?
89. Did you have a piano or a pump organ in your house, as a child?
90. Did you ever take piano lessons or try to teach yourself to play the piano?
91. If so, how good at playing the piano were you?
92. Who were your family's next door neighbors when you were a child?
93. What were your next door neighbors like? Friendly, mean, sociable, reclusive, etc.?

94. How old were your next door neighbors?
95. How often did your family or your next door neighbors visit with each other?
96. Did you ever receive any gifts from your neighbors?
97. If so, what were they?
98. Who would babysit you when your parents weren't home?
99. Who was your favorite babysitter?
100. What kind of games or activities would your babysitter do with you?
101. Who cut your hair, when you were a child?
102. What was your usual style of haircut, when you were little?
103. Did you ever cut your own hair?
104. If so, how did that turn out?
105. How often would your parents take you to get new shoes?
106. Do you remember where your family bought shoes?
107. How would you dress, as a child?
108. Did your family ever home-make any clothing?
109. If so, who made the clothing in your family?
110. If your family home-made clothing, how did they do it?
111. If your family home-made clothing, what materials did they use?
112. If your family bought clothing from a store, which store(s) did your family buy clothing from?
113. On what occasions would you get new clothing or new outfits?
114. What is one article of clothing or style of clothing that you really disliked wearing as a child?
115. Do you remember any words or sayings that were common in your youth that nobody says anymore?
116. Did you have a bed time?
117. If so, what time did you have to be in bed by?
118. How old were you when this bed time was enforced?
119. What was the latest you were ever allowed to stay up?
120. What was the occasion?

121. Did your parents ever employ any comfort touches to soothe you, like scratching your back, rubbing your shoulders, brushing your hair, rocking you back and forth, etc.?
122. Did you like to do any drawing or painting as a child?
123. What did you draw or paint?
124. Did anyone teach you how to draw or paint?
125. If so, whom?
126. Did you like to do any writing as a child?
127. What did you write?
128. Did you ever keep a diary or journal?
129. How long did you keep writing in it for?
130. Do you still have those old journals stored somewhere?
131. Did your household always have a television?
132. If not, when did your family get their first television?
133. Was your first television a black and white set, or a color set?
134. How did you adjust the antenna on the television?
135. How did you have to change the channels on the television your family had? Did you have to move the antenna to change the channel, or was there a twist knob on the television set perhaps?
136. What shows did your family watch on television?
137. What was your favorite show to watch on television?
138. Did anyone ever make video recordings of you and your family when you were young?
139. If so, who recorded those videos?
140. If there are video recordings of you or your family from your younger years, do you know where those recordings are today?
141. Did you ever have a family game night?
142. If so, what games would your family play?
143. How often did you see movies at the theater, as a child?
144. How much did movie tickets cost, when you were little?
145. What was your favorite movie you ever saw in your childhood?
146. Do you remember what was the first movie you ever saw?
147. Did you ever make a fort, or have a secret hiding spot?
148. When did you learn how to swim?

149. Where did you go swimming as a child?

150. Did you ever go fishing or hunting, as a child?

151. Where did you fish or hunt?

152. Whom did you fish or hunt with?

153. What was the biggest fish you ever caught, in your younger days?

154. Do you remember the day when you learned how to ride a bicycle?

155. How did you learn how to ride a bicycle? Did anyone help you?

156. Where did you like to ride your bicycle to?

157. Where was the furthest away from home you ever rode your bicycle?

158. Did you wear any helmet, elbow pads, or knee pads when you rode your bicycle?

159. When was your worst "wipe out" on your bicycle?

160. Did your family ever take vacations together?

161. Where were all the places your family vacationed to?

162. What was your favorite vacation that your family ever took?

163. Where was the farthest away from home that you ever traveled, before your 18th birthday?

164. Did you like to read books, as a child?

165. How often would you read?

166. How often did your parents read to you?

167. What was your favorite book to read, as a child?

168. Did you ever play any tricks or pranks on your parents or siblings?

169. How did your parents discipline you?

170. Did you ever have to return anything that you stole, as a child? How did that happen?

171. What was the biggest fib you ever told, as a child?

172. What was the biggest thing you ever got in trouble for?

173. Did you ever run away or hide from your parents after you had done something wrong?

174. Did you ever tattle on a sibling for something they did wrong? How did they react to that?

175. Did you ever have a sibling or friend who got you into trouble, or who blamed you for something they did?

176. If so, were you still on good terms after that incident?

177. What was your family's policy on certain curse words in your household?

178. How consistently was that policy adhered to?

179. Did you have a list of household chores you had to accomplish every day or week?

180. If so, what were they?

181. Did your assigned chores change when new siblings were added to the family?

182. How so?

183. Did you ever help your dad or mom at their job?

184. Did you have an allowance as a child?

185. If so, how much was it, and when were you given it?

186. What was the biggest amount of money you ever had, as a child?

187. How did you spend your weekends?

188. How did you celebrate birthdays in your family?

189. What was your favorite or most memorable birthday gift you ever received, as a child?

190. What was your least favorite type of birthday gift to receive, when you were little?

191. How did you celebrate Christmas in your family?

192. What was your favorite or most memorable Christmas gift you ever received, as a child?

193. How did you celebrate Thanksgiving in your family?

194. Which Thanksgiving did you celebrate with the largest number of family members and household guests?

195. How did you celebrate Easter in your family?

196. (If the interviewee is American) How did you celebrate the Fourth of July in your family?

197. How did you celebrate on New Year's Day in your family?

198. Were there any holidays that your family celebrated when you were growing up, which most other people don't celebrate?
199. If so, what were they and how were they celebrated?
200. How have the ways you celebrate holidays changed between the time you were a child and now?
201. What is your happiest memory from childhood?
202. What is your saddest memory from childhood?
203. What was the angriest you ever got, as a child?
204. What was the worst injury you ever got, as a child?
205. How did your parents react to the injury?
206. Did you ever get into a physical fight with another child?
207. If so, what caused it and how did it turn out?
208. What is the grossest thing you ever saw or experienced, in your childhood?
209. Did you ever do anything that embarrassed your parents?
210. Did you ever frighten your parents half to death?
211. Did you ever get stricken with poison ivy as a child?
212. If so, how did it happen and how was it remedied?
213. Did you ever get sprayed by a skunk as a child?
214. If so, how did it happen and how was it remedied?
215. What is your scariest memory from childhood?
216. What was the one thing you were always most scared of, as a child?
217. Do you remember any particularly frightening nightmares you had as a child?
218. What are some of your most memorable dreams that you had as a child, either scary or non-scary?
219. Do you remember the name of the dentist you went to, as a child?
220. How did you like that dentist?
221. How did you feel when you went to the dentist's office?
222. Did you ever get cavities in your teeth as a child?
223. Did you get in trouble from your parents when the dentist found a cavity in your teeth?

224. What did you do when you had a loose tooth as a child?
225. Did you ever knock a tooth out by injury?
226. If so, what happened?
227. Who was your family doctor, when you were a child?
228. Did they make house calls or did you go to their clinic?
229. How often did you have to go to the emergency room as a child?
230. What were the causes for having to go there?
231. What are some of the biggest crimes you remember being committed in your community, when you were a child?
232. How did your community treat the criminal who committed that crime?
233. Did you ever have a crime committed against you or your family, when you were a child? Was your house ever robbed, or was anyone ever attacked?
234. What is something that you were just never able to understand, as a child?
235. What is the funniest thing you ever remember saying, as a small child?
236. Did you ever do anything really foolish, as a child?
237. Did one of your siblings ever do anything really foolish?
238. Did you ever win any trophies or awards, as a child?
239. What was your proudest moment from childhood?
240. Which of your siblings did you look up to and want to emulate the most?
241. Why did you look up to that sibling?
242. Do you think any of your younger siblings ever looked up to you and tried to emulate you?
243. Which ones, and how so?
244. What is one thing you wish your parents had done, but they never did or perhaps never had a chance to do?
245. What is one thing you are particularly grateful to your parents for doing?
246. What was your favorite restaurant to eat out at, as a child?
247. Did your family move often, during your childhood?

248. Did you like or dislike moving?
249. Can you remember all the different places you lived, and what years or dates you moved?
250. Which move was the hardest on you?
251. Which move were you most excited and optimistic about?
252. What was the first school you attended?
253. Can you remember the names of all your grade school teachers?
254. What were your favorite subjects in grade school?
255. What were your least favorite subjects in grade school?
256. Did you play any junior sports in grade school?
257. What were your favorite and least favorite sports to play in grade school?
258. Who was the coolest or most popular kid in your class?
259. Why were they so cool or popular?
260. Do you know what ever became of that person?
261. Did you play any musical instruments in a band during grade school?
262. If so, which ones?
263. If you were in a school band, what songs that you played in your school band do you remember the best, or which songs were your favorites to play?
264. Did any of your siblings or cousins go to school with you?
265. If you had siblings or cousins that went to school with you, what classes or school activities did you participate in with them?
266. If you had siblings or cousins that went to school with you, did you spend a lot of time with them?
267. If you were in school during the Cold War, did you ever have a safety drill in case of a Soviet bombing?
268. If so, what did you have to do during the drill?
269. What was one of your favorite class field trips that you took?
270. Were you ever disciplined by a teacher or sent to the principal's office?

271. If so, what happened?
272. How often was your school delayed or cancelled due to snow or other inclement weather?
273. Were you ever prevented from getting to school because of snowy roads or flooded roads?
274. If you lived in a snowy area, what kind of games and activities would you play in the snow?
275. If you lived in a non-snowy area, do you ever remember any rare instance where it actually snowed? Was that the first time you saw snow in real life? What did you do when it snowed?
276. Did you ever experience hurricanes as a child?
277. If so, do you remember living through a particularly intense one?
278. Did you ever see a tornado as a child?
279. If so, what happened?
280. What would you and your family do when the electricity in your house went out, when you were a child?
281. What kind of car(s) did your family have when you were growing up?
282. Do you remember when your family got the car(s)?
283. Do you remember where your family bought the car(s) from?
284. How were those cars different from the cars today?
285. Were you ever prone to getting motion sickness while riding in cars?
286. Did you ever learn how to drive a car?
287. If so, how did you learn?
288. Who taught you how to drive a car?
289. What make and model was the car you learned to drive with?
290. Did you ever do any damage to the car or get in any car accidents?
291. If so, what caused the accident and what happened?
292. What was the make and model of your first car?
293. How was that car different from cars today?
294. Who were your favorite and least favorite high school teachers?

295. Why were those teachers your favorite and least favorite?

296. What were your favorite and least favorite subjects in high school?

297. Why were those subjects your favorite and least favorite?

298. Did you ever act in any school plays or musicals?

299. If so, what was your favorite school play or musical that you acted in?

300. What character did you play in that production?

301. Had you tried out for that particular part, or had you originally tried out for a different part?

302. Do you remember any specific lines you got to say in that play or musical?

303. Do you remember what day you graduated from high school?

304. What was the weather like on the day of your high school graduation?

305. Was your high school graduation an outdoor or an indoor ceremony?

306. How did you feel on your high school graduation day?

307. What did you do on your high school graduation day? Did you have any sort of celebration?

308. Did any of your classmates or people from your town go on to become celebrities?

309. Have you ever been to any class reunions?

310. If so, which ones?

311. About how many of your classmates were at the most recent class reunion?

312. Did you see any of your closest school friends at the most recent class reunion?

313. If so, whom?

314. Did anyone famous ever come through your hometown?

315. Do you remember ever being mentioned in a newspaper, when you were young?

316. If so, what was the occasion?

317. What is one thing you missed out on doing in your childhood that you wish you could go back and do?

318. If you could go back into your past and bring one object back to the present, what would you choose?

319. If you had to sum up your childhood in just one word, what would it be?

Immigration

(Questions to be asked if the interviewee is an immigrant)

1. Do you recall the exact date that you left your old country?
2. What time of day was it when you left?
3. What was the weather like in your old country on the day that you left?
4. What things did you pack, to take with you?
5. After you left your home, did you realize that you had forgotten anything, or do you regret choosing not to take something with you?
6. How did you feel about leaving your home land? How scared, excited, or calm were you?
7. If you were a child when you left your country, did your parents explain to you why your family was moving to a new country?
8. If so, what did they tell you?
9. If your parents or grandparents did not emigrate with you, how did they feel about the fact that you were leaving your home land? Were they happy for you, upset, nervous, or a combination of emotions?
10. If you were married or in a committed relationship when you decided to leave your home land, how did your significant other feel about the decision to emigrate?
11. If you were married or in a committed relationship when you decided to leave your home land, did your significant other emigrate with you, emigrate at a different time, or did you have to leave them behind in the old country?
12. How often had you traveled outside your country, before you emigrated permanently?
13. Had you ever visited your current country, before you immigrated here permanently?
14. What was the last thing you ate before you left your home country?

15. Are there any foods from your home country that you really miss?

16. Which friends did you have to leave behind in your old country?

17. Do you still keep in touch with them?

18. Did you and your family already have relatives or friends in the destination country?

19. Did your relatives or friends who had already immigrated ever write or phone back to you or your family in the old country?

20. If so, what kind of things did they tell you about the new country? Did they encourage you to come join them?

21. How long did you or your family debate whether or not to emigrate before you finally made the decision to do so?

22. What kind of preparations did you or your family have to make, before you emigrated?

23. Did you have to receive any immunizations or undergo any medical procedures before you emigrated?

24. How many languages did you and your family speak in the old country?

25. If you immigrated to a country that spoke a different language, did you start learning the new language before you left?

26. If so, how long had you been practicing learning the new language?

27. Were you practicing the new language because you knew you were going to be emigrating, or did you start learning the new language and afterward decide to immigrate to a country that spoke that language?

28. Did you immigrate by boat, plane, ground vehicle, or by foot?

29. If you left your old country at a seaport or an airport, how long of a journey was it from your house to that port?

30. Were there any friends, relatives, or neighbors there to see you off before you left?

31. Do you remember if any of your loved ones left you with parting words before you went?

32. Did anyone give you a gift before you left?

33. Do you remember any particular scents or smells in the air, just before you left your home land?

34. What kind of sounds were there, just before you left your home land? Was there any music playing?

35. What were you wearing when you left your home country?

36. Did you say your final "good bye" to your home land in any special way?

37. What was the thing that you were most looking forward to about living in the new country?

38. What aspect of the new country were you were most scared or upset about?

39. How many people were traveling in your particular party with you?

40. Roughly how many other people, in total, were in the boat or plane or vehicle or traveling group?

41. What kind of government procedures did you have to go through before you were able to leave your home country?

42. If you emigrated by boat or plane or vehicle, do you remember the name of the transport, or the name of the company that owned the transport?

43. How long of a journey was it from the old country to the new country?

44. Were there any stops or layovers along the way?

45. How spacious were your accommodations during transportation?

46. Did you have to change your outfit along the way, possibly because of changing temperatures or climate?

47. Did anything strange or interesting happen during the journey along the way?

48. Did you get any motion sickness or other types of illness while you were traveling?

49. Do you remember seeing anything really amazing during your journey?

50. Did you ever get temporarily separated from your traveling party along the way?

51. What was the scariest moment of your journey?

52. If your journey was long enough that you had to sleep while traveling, how did you sleep?

53. If you sat in a seat during your journey, what did the seat feel like? Was it comfortable?

54. Do you remember anything you ate along the way? How did it taste?

55. Do you remember any particular scents or smells along the way?

56. Did you lose any possessions during the journey?

57. Did you pick up any souvenirs or new possessions along the way?

58. Did you have to care for any younger siblings, children, or relatives during the journey?

59. Was there ever any inclement weather during the journey? What happened?

60. Was there ever a point when you thought you might not make it to the new country?

61. Did anyone in your traveling party die or get seriously ill along the way?

62. Do you recall any particular strangers who you traveled next to?

63. Did you make any new friends during the journey?

64. If so, how did you meet and start talking?

65. If you made new friends during the journey, who were they and what were they like?

66. If you made new friends during the journey, how long after the journey did you keep in touch with them?

67. What kind of things did you do for entertainment, during the journey?

68. What was the date that you arrived in the new country?

69. What time of day was it when you set foot in the new country?

70. What was the weather like on that day?

71. What were you feeling and thinking when you set foot in the new country?

72. What was your immediate first impression of the new country and its people?

73. Did anything really surprise you about the new country when you got here?

74. Had anyone in your old country told you any strange stories or facts about the new country, but when you arrived you discovered the stories were not true?

75. If so, what were the stories?

76. Do you remember what sounds you heard, when you arrived in the new country?

77. What was the first thing you did when you got to the new country?

78. What was the first thing you said when you got to the new country?

79. Was anyone there to greet you?

80. If so, do you remember what they said to you and your traveling group?

81. Did the people who greeted you give you anything when they met you?

82. Who was the first stranger you spoke to in the new country?

83. What kind of government procedures were you subject to when you arrived in the new country?

84. How well did you speak the language of the new country when you arrived here?

85. Can you estimate how many words or phrases you could speak in the new country's language when you first arrived?

86. Did you phone or write home to anyone when you first arrived?

87. If so, whom did you communicate to, and what did you say?

88. What was the first food you ate in the new country?

89. How did it taste?

90. Did you have any sort of celebration or get-together with other people soon after you arrived?

91. If so, who was there, and what did you do?

92. Where did you sleep, your first night in the new country?

93. How well did you sleep that first night?

94. What was it like your first morning in the new country?

95. What kinds of errands and tasks did you have to take care of, your first day in the new country?

96. What was your early impression of the styles of music in the new country?

97. When you arrived in the new country, did you live in a community of people who had also immigrated from your old country?

98. Are there any aspects of the new country that you still haven't gotten used to?

99. Are there any aspects of the new country that you didn't like at first, but that you later came to enjoy or to be okay with?

100. When you first experienced these things, did you think you would ever get used to them?

101. Was anyone particularly nice or particularly mean to you, when you first arrived?

102. Who was the first new friend you made after you arrived?

103. If you were of working age when you arrived in the new country, did you already have a job waiting for you?

104. What was your first job in the new country?

105. At your first job in the new country, was your employer of the same nationality or ethnicity as you?

106. Did your first employer in your new country also speak your primary language?

107. If you are a naturalized citizen of your present country, how long did it take you to gain citizenship?

108. Can you explain the entire legal process you had to undergo to obtain your present citizenship, green card, etc.?

109. Did you ever have to worry about possibly being deported?

110. Would you recommend other people from your home country to come immigrate to this country too?
111. If you could go back in time, would you still have chosen to immigrate?
112. Why or why not?
113. If you could go back in time, what would you tell your past self before emigrating?
114. What would you say to your child or grandchild if they told you they wanted to immigrate to a different country?
115. What are the biggest differences between your new country and your old country?
116. What lesson could people in your new country learn from the ways of your old country?
117. What lesson could the people in your old country learn from the ways of your new country?
118. How often have you gone back to visit your old country?
119. If you had to sum up your immigration journey in just one word, what would it be?

Jobs and Career

1. When you were a child, what would you say when people asked you, "What do you want to be when you grow up?"

2. Was that what you really wanted to be when you grew up, or did you just tell grownups what you thought they wanted to hear?

3. When you were a child, did anyone (like a parent or a teacher), ever suggest a particular future career to you? Did they ever say, "You should really become a _____ when you grow up, because you're good at _____"?

4. Were there any hobbies you were good at or talents that you've had since you were young, which you could have turned into a career but didn't?

5. Did you ever engage in any childhood entrepreneurial activities before you got your first steady employment? (Such as making a lemonade stand, mowing neighbors' lawns, etc.)

6. Did you ever consider joining the military, but decide against it?

7. Why or why not?

8. Did you ever attempt to join the military but get rejected for a health or medical reason?

9. If so, how did you feel when this happened?

10. Did you ever get a deferment from being drafted into the military?

11. If so, what was the deferment for?

12. Have you ever tried to make a living from any sort of artistic or musical endeavor?

13. If so, what was it, and how did it turn out?

14. If you had a parent or older relative who owned a business, did you ever help them out with that business?

15. What was the first steady employment you ever had?

16. Was it a paid or unpaid position?

17. If your first job was unpaid, what was the first job you ever got paid for?

18. How did you get that first paid job?

19. Did you get your first job because you wanted it, or because your parents made you do it?
20. Do you remember interviewing for your first job?
21. How did the interview go?
22. What was the name of your first employer?
23. What was your first employer like? Were they nice, mean, demanding, easygoing, etc.?
24. What was the nicest thing your employer ever did for you?
25. When did your employer make you the angriest you ever got at him/her?
26. What specifically did your employer do to make you that angry?
27. Who were your coworkers at your first job?
28. What were the coworkers at your first job like?
29. How did you get along with them?
30. How long did you work at your first job?
31. Do you remember the names of any of the most regular customers you served at your first job?
32. What made those customers unique or memorable?
33. Who was your favorite customer at your first job?
34. What was the most difficult task you were ever assigned, at your first job?
35. How did you do at that task?
36. What was your favorite task to be assigned, at your first job?
37. How did you spend your breaks, at your first job?
38. What skills or talents did you pick up at your first job?
39. How did the lessons you learned at your very first job influence how you've worked in your most recent career?
40. How did you quit your first job?
41. Why did you quit your first job?
42. What was your second job?
43. When did you get your second (third, fourth, etc.) job?
44. What was your employer at your second (third, fourth, etc.) job like?

45. What were your coworkers at your second (third, fourth, etc.) job like?

46. What were the customers or clients at your second (third, fourth, etc.) job like?

47. What are some of your fondest memories from your second (third, fourth, etc.) job?

48. What are some of your least fond memories from your second (third, fourth, etc.) job?

49. How did you spend your breaks at your second (third, fourth, etc.) job?

50. How long did you work at your second (third, fourth, etc.) job?

51. How did you quit your second (third, fourth, etc.) job?

52. Why did you quit your second (third, fourth, etc.) job?

53. What important skills or lessons did you pick up from your second (third, fourth, etc.) job?

54. Did anyone ever try to rob or steal from your workplace (whether customer, or employee, or employer)?

55. Did you ever have a customer who didn't pay what they owed?

56. Can you remember a time when you had to deal with an irate customer?

57. If so, did you keep your cool or did you tell them off?

58. How did the irate customer react to your approach?

59. Did you ever embarrass yourself in front of a customer?

60. If so, what happened?

61. Was there ever a time when something happened that caused your workplace to close down and all the employees got to go home early? If so, what happened?

62. Did you ever work at a job that had outside-of-the-workplace activities like a company softball team or company picnics?

63. Who was the best boss you ever had?

64. Why were they such a good boss?

65. What qualities do you think a good boss needs to have?

66. Who was your least favorite boss you ever had?

67. Why did you dislike working for that boss?

68. Have you ever been an employer, or in a position of authority over someone?

69. If you have been a boss, what do you think is the key to managing a successful and efficient workplace?

70. If you have been a boss, what do you think is the key to having happy employees?

71. If you have been a boss, what is one of the toughest decisions you ever had to make?

72. If you have been a boss, did you ever have a disgruntled employee?

73. If so, how did you deal with it?

74. If you have been a boss, have you ever had to fire someone? How did you handle it?

75. If you have been a boss, can you think of what qualities made a really good employee, in your eyes?

76. If you have been a boss, what did you look for in applicants when you interviewed a prospective employee?

77. If you have been a boss, what is the most important lesson you learned from being one?

78. Have you ever started your own business from the ground up?

79. What was the legal process you had to go through, at the time and place that you started your business?

80. If you have started your own business, how did you get the idea for your business?

81. If you have started your own business, how did you get the funding to start it up?

82. If you have started your own business, did it take a lot of discipline to work for yourself or was it easy for you?

83. Have you ever sold a business that you started?

84. If so, how did you feel once you sold it?

85. What is the most important lesson you learned from starting a business?

86. Who were your favorite coworkers you ever worked with? Why?

87. Did you ever have to cover for a coworker who had done something wrong or who needed some help?
88. If so, what happened?
89. Do you ever remember a time when one of your coworkers died?
90. If so, how did your workplace honor them?
91. What was the best piece of advice a boss or coworker ever gave you?
92. What is the most memorable thing a boss or coworker of yours ever said?
93. Did anything really hilarious ever happen to you on the job?
94. What is the strangest job you ever had, or the weirdest thing you ever had to do to earn some money?
95. Did you ever work with a family member?
96. If so, how did you work together as coworkers?
97. When did you know you wanted to work in your most recent career?
98. What attracted you to your most recent job?
99. Do you prefer to work independently, or in groups/teams?
100. Do you prefer to work with your hands, or to work in the realm of ideas?
101. Do you feel like you learn best when you read how to do it, when you see someone else do it, or when you do it yourself?
102. Can you remember a time when your hard work really paid off in a rewarding way?
103. Did you go to any college or occupational training program after high school?
104. If so, where did you attend?
105. What made you choose that particular college or school?
106. Was that the kind of education or training you personally wanted to get, or did you get that kind of education or training because your parents wanted you to?
107. Did you live in dorms, did you live off-campus but independently of your parents, or did you live with your parents while you attended college?

108. If you lived in dorms or had your own apartment/house during college, who were your roommates or housemates?

109. If you had dorm mates or housemates during college, what were they like?

110. If you had dorm mates or housemates during college, who was your favorite dorm mate?

111. Why were they your favorite dorm mate or housemate?

112. If you had dorm mates or housemates, what was the funniest thing you ever did together?

113. If you had dorm mates or housemates, what was the craziest thing you ever did together?

114. Did you ever have a negative experience with any dorm mates or housemates?

115. If so, what happened and how did you resolve it?

116. If you lived with dorm mates or housemates, how long did you do so?

117. Were you ever in a fraternity or sorority during college?

118. If so, which one(s), and for how long?

119. If you were in a college fraternity or sorority, were there any initiation rituals?

120. If so, what were they?

121. If you were in a college fraternity or sorority, what kinds of activities did you do as a group?

122. Is there anything you didn't do during college, but wish you had?

123. If so, what?

124. Is there anything you did during college that you wish you hadn't?

125. If so, what?

126. If you attended college, who was your favorite professor?

127. Why were they your favorite professor?

128. If you attended college, who was your least favorite professor?

129. Why were they your least favorite professor?

130. If you attended college, what was your favorite course that you ever took?

131. Why was that your favorite course?

132. If you attended college, what was your least favorite course that you ever took?

133. Why was that your least favorite course?

134. If you attended college, what is the most important thing you learned from your college career?

135. What advice would you give to young people beginning their college education today?

136. Did you graduate from college with any honors or accolades?

137. Was the career you went to school for the career you actually ended up in?

138. If you didn't end up in the career you went to school for, do you think that original training ended up being a waste of time, or do you think it has still helped you in your current career?

139. If you went to college in your younger years, and you could go back and do it again, would you pick a different degree or program than the one you originally chose?

140. If so, which degree or program would you switch to?

141. Why do you now feel like you should have chosen that degree or program?

142. If you didn't ever go to college, do you wish you would have?

143. Why or why not?

144. How essential do you think college education is to being a successful worker in today's economy?

145. Did you ever try your hand at a job you thought you would be really good at or thought you would really enjoy, only to find out that you were definitely not cut out for it?

146. Has anyone ever tried to deny you a job for a petty reason, on account of something like your ethnicity, your religion, or because someone had a personal vendetta?

147. If so, what happened and how did you react?

148. What was the most frightening moment in your entire work career?

149. Did you ever successfully solve a really big problem at work?

150. If you worked in sales, can you remember your biggest and/or most successful sale?

151. What was your proudest moment in your working career?

152. What is the biggest mistake you ever made at work? What happened?

153. Did you ever take a really fun business-related trip?

154. If so, where was it to?

155. Why was that business-related trip so enjoyable?

156. Did you ever enter a career to follow in a parent's footsteps or in an older relative's footsteps?

157. What is your secret to balancing work life and home/family life?

158. Were you ever a stay-at-home parent or homemaker?

159. If so, were you always a stay-at-home parent or homemaker?

160. Did you leave a paid career to become a stay-at-home parent or homemaker?

161. If so, what prompted you to do that?

162. Are you glad you did that, or do you wish you would have chosen differently?

163. Did having children create any changes in your career path? How so?

164. Did you leave behind being a stay-at-home parent or homemaker in order to get a paid job?

165. If so, what prompted you to do that?

166. Are you glad you did that, or do you wish you would have chosen differently?

167. If you were a stay-at-home parent or homemaker, have you always felt appreciated and respected, or have you ever felt like sometimes other people don't understand what you go through?

168. If you were a stay-at-home parent or homemaker, what was your typical day's schedule like?

169. Do you have any tips or tricks for grocery shopping and cooking meals on a budget?

170. Did you ever get behind on your bills when you were starting off in life?

171. Did anyone ever help you out when you hit rough times financially?

172. What is the highest number of jobs you've ever had to work at the same time?

173. Was it really stressful, or did you enjoy keeping busy?

174. Did you ever have to work and go to school simultaneously?

175. If so, how was that? Did one affect the other?

176. Have you ever bought a house, rather than rented?

177. If so, what was the first house that you ever bought?

178. If you've bought a house, where was it?

179. If you've bought a house, how big was it?

180. If you've bought a house, what did it look like?

181. How did it feel to own a house?

182. Do you prefer owning or renting?

183. What advice would you give to someone who is trying to decide whether to rent or own?

184. Have you ever built a house?

185. If so, how did the construction process go?

186. If you've had a house built, how did you decide on the layout and architecture?

187. If you've had a house built, what were some of the biggest advantages of doing so?

188. If you've had a house built, what were some of the biggest challenges you faced?

189. If you've had a house built, how did the end product compare with your expectations?

190. Are you glad that you had a house built, or do you wish you would have gotten an already existing home?

191. What advice would you give to someone who is trying to decide whether to build a house, or to acquire an already existing home?

192. Were you ever unemployed and unable to find any work at all?
193. How did you feel when you were out of a job?
194. If you could have any job or career you wanted, what would it be?
195. Why would you enjoy that job or career?
196. Is there any job you're especially glad you've never had to do?
197. What career advice would you give to your children and grandchildren?
198. If you could sum up your career in one word, what would it be?

Likes and Dislikes

1. What are your favorite foods or meals?
2. What are your least favorite foods or meals?
3. What are some of your favorite recipes to make?
4. Do you prefer having a large midday meal and a small evening meal, or a small midday meal and a large evening meal?
5. What is your favorite restaurant to eat out at?
6. Why do you like that restaurant so much?
7. Have you ever had a really bad experience at a restaurant?
8. If so, what happened?
9. How much do you think it is appropriate to tip a waiter or waitress?
10. Do you prefer tea, coffee, or neither?
11. How do you take your tea/coffee?
12. What is your favorite flavor of ice cream?
13. What is your least favorite flavor of ice cream?
14. Do you like pizza?
15. If so, what is your favorite topping?
16. Are there any two foods you like to combine, but other people think it's strange?
17. Do you like spicy foods?
18. Do you like sweet foods?
19. What is your favorite dessert?
20. Do you drink soda?
21. If so, what are your favorite and least favorite brands of soda?
22. Do you say "soda," "pop," "coke," or "sodapop"?
23. Do you drink alcohol?
24. If so, what kind of alcoholic beverages do you prefer?
25. Do you smoke?
26. If so, how often do you smoke?
27. If you smoke, what do you prefer to smoke?
28. What is your favorite color?
29. Do you have a favorite type of flower?
30. Do you enjoy gardening?

31. Which of the four seasons is your favorite?
32. Why do you like that season the most?
33. Which of the four seasons do you least look forward to?
34. Why do you dislike that season?
35. What is your favorite type of car?
36. Can you play any musical instruments?
37. If so, which ones?
38. How and when did you learn to play those instruments?
39. When, where, and why did you purchase or receive your musical instruments?
40. What songs are you the best at playing, or are your favorite to play?
41. What are your favorite genres of music?
42. Do you have any favorite musical performers or groups?
43. What are your least favorite genres of music?
44. What is your favorite show to watch on television?
45. Are there any television shows you can't stand?
46. What genres of television shows do you like the most?
47. What genres of television shows do you like the least?
48. What is your favorite movie?
49. Did you ever see a movie that was just terrible?
50. If so, what was it?
51. What genres of movies do you like the most?
52. What genres of movies do you like the least?
53. Have you ever fantasized about being a movie star or a famous actor?
54. If so, what kind of films would you like to act in, and what kind of role would you like to play?
55. Which movie star(s) have you fantasized about being?
56. What are your favorite board games or card games to play?
57. What do you feel is so fun about those games?
58. Which board games or card games do you dislike playing?
59. Why do you dislike them?

60. What are some of your favorite books or authors that you've ever read?

61. Are there any books you've read that you found really boring?

62. What is something that you really like, but very few other people like?

63. What is something that you really dislike, but everybody else seems to like?

64. What is your favorite outfit or article of clothing to wear?

65. What is one article of clothing you dislike wearing, or a style of outfit that you wouldn't be caught dead in?

66. When you need to relax, what do you do?

67. What is your favorite way to spend a weekend?

68. What is something you never look forward to?

69. What is something that really stresses you out?

70. What is your idea of perfect weather?

71. What do you typically do when the electricity in your home goes out?

72. Where is your favorite place you ever lived?

73. Why did you like it so much?

74. Where is your least favorite place you ever lived?

75. Why did you dislike it?

76. If you could live anywhere in the world, where would you want to live?

77. If you were stranded on a desert island and could have only five things, what would they be?

78. If you were stranded on a desert island and could have only one thing, what would it be?

79. Do you think we should get rid of a lot of our technology and return to simpler times?

80. Why do you feel that way?

81. Would you be content, living without any electricity or running water?

82. Would you rather live in a close-knit community where everybody knew everything about you, or would you rather live all by yourself in a cabin in the woods?

83. When you are on vacation, do you prefer camping out or staying in a hotel?
84. Why do you prefer that?
85. Where is the best place you've ever vacationed?
86. What did you do there?
87. Why did you like it so much?
88. What was the worst vacation you ever took?
89. Why did you dislike it?
90. Where would you like to visit that you still haven't been?
91. If you could vacation anywhere in the world for free, where would you want to vacation?
92. Is there any place on Earth that you definitely never want to visit?
93. What is your favorite sport to watch and/or play?
94. What is your favorite scent?
95. Besides your spouse, who are your closest friends in the world?
96. What is your favorite saying, quote, or word of wisdom?
97. What is the dumbest thing you ever heard anybody say?
98. What unique words or catchphrases do you find yourself saying all the time?
99. What is your preferred way of cooling off in hot weather?
100. What is your preferred way of keeping warm in cold weather?
101. What is your favorite eye color?
102. What is your favorite hair color?
103. What is your favorite type of animal?
104. What is your favorite type of pet to have?
105. What was the best pet you ever had?
106. Did you ever have a pet that you didn't like?
107. Are you afraid of heights?
108. Are you afraid of the dark?
109. Are you afraid of snakes, spiders, bugs, or mice?
110. Have you ever had to take care of a bug or a pest, for someone who was afraid but was much bigger and stronger than you?
111. What are your biggest fears?

112. Would you rather be rich, or live a simple life?

113. What is the most valuable thing you've ever owned?

114. Would you rather live in a big house with lots of space, or a small house without a lot of possessions?

115. When you find something that's not useful to you right now, are you more inclined to get rid of it to keep down on clutter, or are you more inclined to stash it away somewhere in case you might need it in the future?

116. Would you rather live in a big city, in a small town, or in the countryside?

117. Do you prefer carpeting or hardwood floors?

118. Do you prefer painted walls, wood-paneled walls, or wallpaper?

119. Do you prefer modern styles or antique styles?

120. Do you have a favorite piece of furniture or piece of décor?

121. Do you have a piece of furniture that you've never really liked, but have never been able to get rid of?

122. How often should a house be dusted and vacuumed?

123. Do you consider yourself more outgoing, or more shy?

124. Would you prefer going out with friends on a Friday night, or staying in and watching television?

125. Do you like having your picture taken?

126. Would you rather read a book, or would you rather do something with your hands?

127. What do you enjoy doing for physical exercise?

128. If you could be any superhero, who would you be?

129. Why would you choose that superhero?

130. If you could have any superpower, what would it be?

131. Why would you choose that superpower?

132. Would you want to be able to read other people's minds, if you could?

133. Why or why not?

134. Do you have an opinion on how mothers should give birth to children? (i.e. hospital birth, home birth, water birth, with midwife, with pain killers, without pain killers, etc.)

135. Why do you have that opinion?

136. Do you think children should be encouraged to ask questions and express themselves, or do you think children should be seen and not heard?
137. Why do you feel that way?
138. Do you think children these days are better or worse behaved than they were when you were a child?
139. If you think a change has occurred over time, why do you think it has happened?
140. What do you think about most parents' parenting techniques in this day and age?
141. Do you enjoy challenging yourself to learn how to use new technologies?
142. Why or why not?
143. Do you enjoy doing any art, like drawing, painting, sculpting, weaving, knitting, embroidering, etc.?
144. Why do you enjoy art so much or so little?
145. If something is broken, would you rather hire a professional to fix it, or would you rather try to fix it yourself?
146. Why do you feel that way?
147. When you buy something in a box, do you start putting it together right away or do you read the instructions first?
148. Should women have long hair, or short hair?
149. Why do you prefer that length of hair?
150. Should men have a beard, or should they be clean shaven?
151. Why do you like or dislike beards?
152. What temperature do you keep your thermostat set at?
153. What is your favorite holiday to celebrate?
154. Why is that your favorite holiday?
155. What is your least favorite holiday?
156. Why is that your least favorite holiday?
157. What time do you prefer to go to bed?
158. Why do you like to go to bed at that time?
159. Do you prefer to sleep on a firm bed, or a soft bed?

160. Do you prefer to sleep on top of your covers or underneath them?

161. Do you like to sleep in a cool room or a warm room?

162. What time do you prefer to wake up?

163. Why do you prefer to wake up at that time?

164. When you are doing work, does it help you to have complete silence or does it help you to have music playing in the background?

165. Why do you prefer silence or background music while you work?

166. If you prefer to play music in the background while you work, what kind of music?

167. What is your favorite day of the week?

168. Why is that your favorite day?

169. What are some of your favorite jokes that you've ever heard?

170. Do you like to tell jokes?

171. What joke do you like to tell the most?

172. Do you ever walk, jog, or run, just for fun or exercise?

173. What is the furthest you ever remember walking on foot?

174. If you had one million dollars to spend, what would you do with it?

175. Do you ever gamble?

176. Why or why not?

177. If you do gamble, do you gamble at home, at friends' houses, at casinos, at a bingo hall, somewhere else, or all of the above?

178. Do you ever play the lottery or buy scratch tickets?

179. Why or why not?

180. Have you ever won anything in a lottery or a scratch ticket?

181. If so, what did you win?

182. What do you think is the key to a healthy, long life?

183. If you could sum up your personality in one word, what would it be?

Love, Marriage & Family

1. Who was your first boyfriend or girlfriend?
2. Where would you and your boyfriend(s) or girlfriend(s) typically go on dates?
3. Did you ever date anyone against your parents' wishes?
4. If so, why did you do it, and how did it turn out?
5. Did you ever have any difficult breakups with a boyfriend or girlfriend?
6. If so, do you remember why you broke up?
7. If you had a difficult breakup, how did it make you feel?
8. Did you ever think, after a breakup, that you would never find true love again?
9. How were you eventually consoled after the difficult breakup(s)?
10. Was there ever a time in your youth when you thought you didn't ever want to get married?
11. Why or why not?
12. How did you meet your spouse?
13. Did anyone introduce you and your spouse or set you up?
14. Were you friends with your spouse before you started dating?
15. Was your family acquainted with your spouse's family before marriage?
16. Did anyone else from your immediate or extended family marry anyone else from your spouse's immediate or extended family?
17. How far apart did you and your future spouse live from one another before you started dating?
18. Was it love at first sight when you met your future spouse, or did they grow on you?
19. Had your future spouse previously dated one of your friends before they started dating you?
20. What was the first date you went on with your spouse?
21. Who asked whom on the date, and how did they ask?

22. Did you or your spouse ever previously attempt to ask the other person out on a date, but got too nervous and couldn't ask?

23. Did you or your spouse ever attempt to ask the other person out on a date before, but one of you turned the other one down at first?

24. If so, why?

25. What was the most fun date you ever had with your future spouse?

26. Did you and your future spouse ever go to any movies together?

27. If so, did you ever see any scary movies?

28. If so, did you use the scary scenes as an excuse hold on to your future spouse?

29. What is the funniest thing that ever happened on one of your dates?

30. Did you ever accidentally make a fool of yourself in front of your future spouse?

31. Did your future spouse ever accidentally make a fool of themselves in front of you?

32. What qualities in your spouse attracted you to them?

33. What qualities did your spouse say attracted them to you?

34. What interests or hobbies did you and your future spouse have in common with each other?

35. What were the biggest differences you had with your future spouse?

36. Were you and your future spouse both of the same religious persuasion?

37. If not, what were your differences?

38. If not, how did you reconcile these differences?

39. Do you think your religious differences have strengthened your relationship, or do you think they were a challenge that had to be overcome?

40. Were you and your future spouse both of the same political opinions?

41. If not, what were your differences?

42. If not, how did you reconcile these differences?
43. Do you think your political differences have strengthened your relationship, or do you think they were a challenge that had to be overcome?
44. Were you and your future spouse both of the same ethnicity or national origin?
45. Were you and your future spouse both from the same economic background? Did one of you come from a significantly poorer or wealthier background than the other?
46. Did your different backgrounds pose any challenges to your relationship?
47. When you started dating your future spouse, did your parents get along well with their parents?
48. Did you and your future spouse ever have any big disagreements or fights when you were dating?
49. If so, what was it about?
50. When you and your future spouse were young and dating, how would you handle disagreements in general? What would you and your future spouse do when one of you was angry at the other?
51. When did your parents find out that you and your future spouse were a couple?
52. How did your parents react?
53. How did your best friend react when they found out that you and your future spouse were a couple?
54. How did you first introduce your future spouse to your parents?
55. What kind of first impression did your future spouse make on your parents?
56. What happened when your future spouse first introduced you to their parents?
57. What kind of first impression do you think you made on your future parents-in-law?

58. Did anyone else ever try unsuccessfully to steal your heart from your future spouse, or did anyone else every try unsuccessfully to steal your future spouse away from you?

59. If so, what happened?

60. Were you and your future spouse ever separated by a long distance for a significant length of time?

61. How did you communicate with your future spouse during that time?

62. How long did you date your spouse before you got engaged?

63. How did you and your spouse become engaged?

64. Who proposed to whom?

65. How did the proposer ask the question, and what were the words that the other person said in response?

66. Did you and your spouse discuss getting married before you actually got engaged, or was the proposal a complete surprise?

67. Did you ever live with your spouse before getting married?

68. If so, how long did you live together?

69. If you lived with your spouse before marriage, how did that influence your decision to marry them?

70. Would you recommend that couples should or should not live together before marriage?

71. On what day did you marry your spouse?

72. What building or location did you marry your spouse in, and in what city?

73. What time of day was your wedding ceremony?

74. What was the weather like on your wedding day?

75. What emotions were you feeling on the morning of your wedding day?

76. Do you remember any particular scents in the air on your wedding day?

77. What music was played at your wedding ceremony?

78. Did anything funny happen, or did anyone say anything memorably funny, on your wedding?

79. Where was your wedding reception held, and when?

80. Did you have a live band play at your wedding reception?

81. If so, what kind of music did the band play?
82. Did anyone give any speeches at your wedding reception?
83. If so, who spoke?
84. If anyone gave any speeches at your wedding reception, do you remember anything in particular that was said in these speeches?
85. Did you have a wedding ceremony, or did you elope?
86. If you eloped, how long did each of you wait to tell your parents?
87. What did your parents say when you told them that you had eloped?
88. Did you have more than one wedding ceremony, or have you ever had a recommitment ceremony?
89. If so, when and where was this second ceremony, and why did you choose to have it?
90. Do you remember what wedding presents you and your spouse received, and from whom?
91. Where did you and your spouse go for your honeymoon?
92. How long did you stay on your honeymoon?
93. Did any other friends or family members join you on your honeymoon?
94. Have you ever been at a wedding where the officiator asked, "If anyone knows any reason why these two should not be wed, speak now or forever hold your peace," and somebody actually spoke up?
95. If so, what was said and what happened?
96. Where did you and your spouse make your first home, once you were married?
97. Can you describe the first house or apartment that you and your spouse lived in together?
98. Can you describe the neighborhood that you and your spouse first lived in together after marriage?
99. Do you remember who your next door neighbors were at the first place you and your spouse lived after marriage?

100. What is the longest amount of time you and your spouse ever had to go without seeing one another?
101. How did you feel after going that long without seeing your spouse?
102. What advice would you give to anyone who wants to be happy in their marriage?
103. When did you first realize that you or your spouse was pregnant with your first child?
104. How did you feel when you found out?
105. How did your spouse react when they found out?
106. How difficult or easy was the first pregnancy?
107. Do you remember any particular difficulties or challenges you had to overcome during the pregnancy?
108. Was a baby shower ever thrown?
109. If so, who hosted it, and who attended?
110. Do you remember the moment when you or your spouse realized that the time had arrived for the baby to be born?
111. If so, who said what, and what happened?
112. Would you have had more children, if you could have?
113. What is your opinion on pregnancy out of wedlock?
114. How important or unimportant do you feel it is that a couple be married when their child is born?
115. When you were growing up, how did people in your family react when they knew of someone who was pregnant out of wedlock?
116. When you were growing up, how did people in your community react when they knew of someone who was pregnant out of wedlock?
117. When you were growing up, how did people in your community react when someone bore a child out of wedlock?
118. When you were growing up, how did people in your family react when someone bore a child out of wedlock?
119. What methods of discipline did you use with your children?
120. What methods of discipline on children do you think are appropriate, and what methods are inappropriate?

121. What was the time one of your children frightened you the most?

122. What was the time one of your children infuriated you the most?

123. What are the funniest things your children ever said or did?

124. What are some of the sweetest things your children have ever done for you?

125. Has one of your children ever taught you an important lesson? What was it?

126. How did you choose to instill a work ethic in your children?

127. What did you do for your children when they were sick? Any special remedies?

128. Which do you think has more of a positive effect on a child? Encouraging them verbally and showing them affection, or providing for their physical needs and making sure they have a decent education?

129. What do you think is the ideal number of children to have?

130. Why do you have that opinion?

131. Does parenting get harder or easier, the older you get?

132. Why do you feel that way?

133. What, in your opinion, is the ideal age to have a first child?

134. Why do you feel that way?

135. What, in your opinion, is the best age to be a parent?

136. Why do you feel that way?

137. What special dish or meal do you cook that you are "famous" for in your family?

138. Is there anyone alive today who you haven't seen in a long time that you would like to see at least one more time?

139. What do you think true love means?

140. What does it mean to forgive someone?

141. Have you ever had to forgive someone who did something really wrong to you?

142. If so, are you able to talk at all about what happened?

143. Has anyone ever forgiven you for doing something really wrong that you did to them?

144. If so, are you able to talk at all about what happened?

145. Where do you consider to be your "home town"?

146. What is your proudest accomplishment as a spouse and/or a parent?

147. If you could sum up your marriage in one word, what would it be?

Military Service

1. When did you make the decision that you wanted to join the military?
2. How old were you at the time when you came to this decision?
3. What made you want to join the military?
4. Which branch of the military did you originally join?
5. Why did you choose that branch?
6. Did you have any relatives or friends who had previously joined the military?
7. Did their decision to join influence your decision to join?
8. What was the day when you actually signed on the dotted line to join the military?
9. Do you remember what the building was like, where you signed up for the military?
10. Do you remember who the recruiter was, or what kind of person they were like?
11. How did you feel at the moment when you officially signed up?
12. Did you sign up with any friends or relatives?
13. If so, whom?
14. Was there any active war going on at the time you joined the military, or was there any sort of imminent threat of war at the time?
15. If so, how did the national situation influence your decision to join? Did it make you more willing to join, or more apprehensive about joining perhaps?
16. How did your friends feel about your decision to join the military?
17. How did your family members feel about your decision to join the military?
18. Did you have a significant other at the time you decided to join the military?
19. If so, how did they feel about this decision?

20. Did you have to make any sacrifices in order to join the military?

21. If so, what were they?

22. Were you drafted/conscripted into the military?

23. If so, so you remember the day when you received the notice that you had been drafted?

24. If you were drafted, in what way did you first find out that you had been drafted? Did you receive a letter in the mail, or did you read your draft number printed in a newspaper perhaps?

25. If you were drafted, how did you initially feel upon finding out that you had been drafted?

26. If you were drafted, what did you do when you found out that you had been drafted?

27. If you were drafted, do you remember what was happening on the day when you found you had been drafted?

28. What was the weather like on the day you were drafted?

29. What was everyone doing, on the day you were drafted?

30. If you were drafted, how did your friends and loved ones react when they found out you had been drafted?

31. Did you ever know anyone who attempted to escape the draft?

32. If so, what happened to them?

33. If you knew someone who attempted to escape the draft, how did people treat them?

34. Did you have to go through many medical and health examinations in the sign-up process?

35. Were there any medical problems or issues you had that almost disqualified you from joining?

36. If so, what were they?

37. If you had to overcome any medical or health issues to join the military, how did you clear those issues?

38. Did the military recruiter ever make any promises to you that weren't kept?

39. How long of a wait was there between the time you signed up and the time you went off to basic training?

40. What did you do during the weeks between sign-up and basic training?
41. Do you remember the day when you went to basic training?
42. Did anybody see you off, when you left?
43. If so, who saw you off?
44. Did anybody leave any parting words or advice with you before you went off to basic training?
45. If so, who told you what?
46. How were you transported from your hometown to the basic training camp?
47. Do you remember what you were thinking about on the journey to the basic training camp?
48. If you were traveling to basic training with other people, what were they doing during the journey?
49. Did you talk to anyone while traveling to your basic training camp?
50. If so, did you meet any new people that you formed friendships with?
51. If so, who were they?
52. What day and time of day did you arrive at the basic training camp?
53. What was the weather like at the time you arrived?
54. Who greeted you when you arrived at the basic training camp? Was it a drill sergeant?
55. What was said to you when you first arrived?
56. How did you feel when you first set foot on the basic training camp grounds?
57. What sort of routines did you have to go through when you first arrived at basic training?
58. What time were you finally able to get to bed that first night?
59. What was going through your mind at the end of the first night of basic training?
60. Did you sleep well that first night?

61. Do you remember who your bunk mates or cabin mates were at basic training?
62. Who was your drill sergeant?
63. What was your drill sergeant like?
64. What was the training you went through during basic training, and when did you receive each type of training chronologically?
65. What was the most difficult point of your basic training?
66. How was the reality of basic training different from the expectations that you had had beforehand?
67. Was there ever a point during basic training when you thought you weren't going to make it?
68. If so, what happened and how did you overcome it?
69. Was there a point in your basic training when you got used to the experience, and felt like you were going to make it?
70. If so, what happened?
71. What was your proudest or greatest moment from basic training?
72. Did you ever receive any injuries during basic training?
73. If so, what happened?
74. What was the worst injury that anyone in your group of cadets ever received during basic training?
75. What happened and how was it dealt with?
76. What was your most embarrassing moment from basic training?
77. Did the actions of any one individual in your basic training group ever incur a punishment on the entire group?
78. If so, what happened?
79. If so, how did all the other cadets respond to the individual who had incurred the group punishment?
80. What is the riskiest or most foolhardy thing you ever did during basic training?
81. What is the funniest thing that ever happened during basic training?
82. Did you make any lifelong friends during basic training?
83. What kind of recreational activities would you do during your free time, during basic training?

84. What was the most important lesson you learned during basic training?

85. Do you remember the day when you graduated from basic training?

86. What was the weather like on graduation day?

87. How did you feel on graduation day?

88. Did you enter the military enlisted, or as an officer?

89. What rank or pay-grade did you start off at?

90. What job had you originally signed up for in the military?

91. Was that the job you had initially wanted to get?

92. After graduating from basic training, was that the job that you actually got, or did you end up being assigned to a different job?

93. What was the first base or installation that you were stationed at, after basic training?

94. How did you like the first job you were assigned to?

95. What was the city or area like where you were first stationed? Was there anything fun to do in the area?

96. What kind of recreational activities would you do during your free time, at the first place you were stationed at?

97. How long were you stationed at this first location?

98. How did you feel when it came time to leave this first location and get stationed to another location?

99. Did you have any say in where you got stationed for the second location?

100. Where are all the places you have been stationed at or deployed to during your military career, and when were you stationed there?

101. If you had your own family while you were in the military, were your spouse and children with you when you were stationed at these places?

102. If not, where were they?

103. What was your favorite place you were ever stationed?

104. Why was that your favorite place?

105. What was your least favorite place you were ever stationed?

106. Why was that your least favorite place?

107. Is there a place you always wish you could have gotten stationed at, but were never able to?

108. Where would that be?

109. If you had a spouse and/or children living with you during your military career, what were their favorite and least favorite places to be stationed?

110. Were you ever assigned to kitchen duty?

111. If so, was it your choice to do it?

112. If you were ever assigned to kitchen duty, how did you like it?

113. What are all the different jobs you have had throughout your military career, and when did you have them?

114. How many overseas locations have you been in, during your military career?

115. Did you ever get to serve in the same unit with, or at the same location as, any friends or relatives?

116. What kind of education and training did you receive throughout your military career?

117. Did you ever coincidentally cross paths with any old friends or relatives while you were serving?

118. Did you ever receive any memorable letters or care packages while deployed?

119. Did you ever celebrate a holiday, like Christmas or your birthday, while deployed and away from family?

120. If so, how did you celebrate it?

121. Did you ever see combat, during your military career?

122. If so, did it consist of formal battles or was the violence more intermittent?

123. Can you recount the specific battles or instances of combat that you experienced?

124. Can you recall the cleverest or most ingenious military maneuver you witnessed during the war?

125. What would you consider to have been the biggest military blunder you witnessed during the war?

126. What was the most harrowing or dangerous moment in your military career?
127. Did you ever fear for your life in that moment?
128. What thoughts went through your mind during those dangerous moments?
129. Did you ever have to fire a weapon at an enemy combatant?
130. If so, how did you feel, the first time you had to do so?
131. What do you feel like the differences were in the mentality of the enemy vs. the mentality of your country's soldiers?
132. Were you ever surprised by any unexpected similarities between enemy combatants and your country's soldiers?
133. Do you ever remember a moment when an enemy combatant showed unexpected mercy to you or one of your comrades, or do you ever remember a moment when you unexpectedly showed mercy to an enemy combatant?
134. If you served during war time, what is the most important lesson you learned about war?
135. Was there ever a moment when you regretted joining the military?
136. If so, what caused you to have second thoughts?
137. If you ever regretted joining the military, what did you do about those feelings?
138. What promotions and medals did you earn, during your military career?
139. What were the medals awarded for?
140. How many years did you spend in the military, in total?
141. When did you decide to get out of the military?
142. What reasons did you have for getting out of the military?
143. How did you feel on your very last day as a member of the military?
144. Did you do anything special on your last day in the military?
145. How did the reality of serving in the military compare to your expectations of the military before you joined?

146. What is the most important life lesson you learned during your whole military career?
147. Would you recommend any of your children or grandchildren to join the military?
148. Why or why not?
149. If you could sum up your military career in just one word, what would it be?

Politics and Spirituality

1. Are you registered with a particular political party?
2. Why do you like that political party?
3. When did you join that political party?
4. Did both of your parents belong to that political party?
5. If not, what were their political persuasions?
6. Did all of your grandparents belong to that political party?
7. If not, do you know what their political persuasions were?
8. Regardless of your political party, what type of political philosophy do you mainly adhere to? (i.e. conservative, liberal, socialist, moderate, centrist, libertarian, anarchist, etc.)
9. Do you feel like your political party is living up to the principles that cause you to identify with the party?
10. Why or why not?
11. If you are not registered with any particular political party, why are you not?
12. How proud do you feel to be a citizen or resident of the country you now live in?
13. Why do you feel that way?
14. How proud do you feel to have been born in the country you now live in?
15. Why do you feel that way?
16. Do you remember the first politician you ever cast a vote for? Who was it?
17. What caused you to vote for that politician?
18. Are you proud of that first vote, or do you regret it?
19. Do you feel like people respect the president (or prime minister) more or less today than they did in your younger years?
20. If you feel like there has been a change over the years in people's respect or disrespect for the president (or prime minister), do you think this change is a good thing or a bad thing?

21. Why do you feel this way?
22. What is the appropriate way to question or criticize an authority figure, whether governmental, religious, etc.?
23. Is there ever a legitimate place for disobeying the orders of a government leader or a commanding officer? Where should one draw the line?
24. What is your opinion of the current president (or prime minister)?
25. Why do you feel that way?
26. Do you think that, in general, the presidency (or the office of the prime minister) has too much power, in this day and age?
27. What is your opinion of the current congress (or parliament)?
28. Why do you feel that way?
29. What is your opinion on the present state of affairs in this country? Are we headed in the right or wrong direction?
30. Do you believe in conscription? Do you think young people should be drafted into the military or into any sort of national service?
31. Why or why not?
32. What is your opinion on so-called "draft dodgers". Do you think they are principled or cowardly?
33. Do you think that, as long as there is a draft, females should also be subject to the draft?
34. Why or why not?
35. Do you think that war, in general, is an acceptable, necessary, or useful tool for a government?
36. Which wars do you think were necessary or a good idea, and why?
37. Which wars do you think were unnecessary or a bad idea, and why?
38. What kind of military presence do you think your nation's government should have around the world?
39. What responsibilities or obligations do you think your nation's government has to the rest of the world?

40. What role(s) and responsibilities should a government have to its own citizens, in your opinion?

41. If a government employee thinks that the government is secretly doing something immoral or illegal, do you think that government employee should blow the whistle and let others know what the government is doing, or do you think that government employee should maintain the government's confidentiality and not leak any top secret information?

42. Is burning your government's flag in protest a form of free expression, or should there be a legal punishment for burning a flag?

43. If you think there should be a legal punishment for burning a flag, what should the punishment be?

44. Do you think there should be any exceptions to the freedom of speech and freedom of the press?

45. If so, what exceptions should there be?

46. Do you think there should be any exceptions to the freedom of religion?

47. If so, what exceptions should there be?

48. What role should the government have in regulating the nation's education system?

49. Do you believe that human pollution is causing the world to get warmer?

50. Why or why not?

51. Do you believe that global warming is a problem that humans need to solve? Why or why not?

52. Do you think that we have any responsibilities to keep the environment clean?

53. If so, what kinds of responsibilities?

54. What role should the government have in keeping the environment clean?

55. Do you believe that marijuana should be legal for consumption? Why or why not?

56. Do you think there is too much consumerism and materialism these days, or do you think that most people have a good balance?

57. What role should the government have in regulating private businesses?

58. What role should the government have in providing social welfare to those who are struggling financially?

59. What is your opinion of Franklin Roosevelt's New Deal program?

60. What is your position on the issue of whether abortion should be legal or not?

61. If you believe in the soul, when do you believe that a human being has a soul? At the moment of conception, sometime during the pregnancy, or at the moment of birth, perhaps?

62. Do you believe it is ever acceptable for a person to kill an innocent human?

63. Do you believe it is ever acceptable for a person to kill an innocent human being, even when the death is collateral damage during wartime?

64. What is your opinion on Harry Truman's atomic bombing of Hiroshima and Nagasaki, during World War 2?

65. Do you believe that governments should have nuclear weapons?

66. Do you believe that individuals should be allowed to own and use guns?

67. What restrictions, if any, do you believe there should be on gun ownership?

68. Have you ever owned any guns?

69. If so, what kinds of guns?

70. Have you ever used a gun for any reason?

71. Have you ever had to use a gun for personal protection, either to scare away or to incapacitate a criminal?

72. If so, what happened?

73. Have you ever owned any weapons besides firearms?

74. If so, what kinds of weapons?

75. Have you ever had to use a weapon other than a firearm for any reason?

76. If so, what happened?

77. What is your view of the police, in general?

78. Do you think that police in your country, over the last several decades, have become too aggressive, or over-militarized?

79. Do you think people in your country, in general, are politically aware enough, or do you think most people in your country are ill informed about politics and current events?

80. Why do you think this is the case?

81. Do you see any need, in your country's future, for another revolution against our own government?

82. Why or why not?

83. If you do see a need for another revolution, how distantly in the future do you see this revolution occurring?

84. If your state or province announced tomorrow that they were breaking away from the federal government to form their own country, how would you react?

85. Why would you react that way?

86. If your county or city or announced tomorrow that they were breaking away from the state or provincial government to form their own state or province, how would you react?

87. Why would you react that way?

88. Do you think racism is still a problem in your country?

89. Why do you feel that way?

90. Would you still be friends with someone if you found out that they were a racist?

91. Why or why not?

92. Have you ever had a close friend who was of a different race than you?

93. If so, did you ever discuss the issue of racism with them?

94. If so, what opinions did you two have on the matter?

95. Were you or anyone in your family ever involved in the Civil Rights Movement?

96. If you weren't actively involved in the Civil Rights Movement, did you believe in the goals of the movement?
97. Why or why not?
98. What is your opinion on the immigration situation in your country?
99. Why do you feel that way?
100. Have you ever written an opinion piece or a letter to the editor and had it published in the newspaper?
101. If so, what was your article about?
102. If you've had a piece published in the newspaper, what newspaper was it printed in?
103. If you've had a piece published in the newspaper, how long ago was it printed?
104. If you had to pick one political leader, from all of history, who best embodied all the political ideals you hold dear, whom would it be?
105. Why would you pick that individual?
106. If you could sum up your political worldview in just one word, what would it be?
107. What religious worldview (or lack thereof) were you raised in?
108. Did you attend any organized religious meetings (at a church, mosque, synagogue, temple, etc.) as a child?
109. How did you feel during those religious gatherings?
110. Do you currently believe in a divine being?
111. If so, what kind of divine being(s)?
112. If you had to define the word "god," how would you do so?
113. Do you believe in an afterlife?
114. If so, what kind of afterlife?
115. Do you believe everyone experiences the same afterlife, or do some people experience a different afterlife than others?
116. Would you use the word "religious" to describe yourself?
117. Would you use any particular ideological label to describe your opinions on the supernatural (such as "Christian," "Muslim," "Jewish," "Buddhist," "Hindu," "pagan," "atheist," "agnostic," etc.)?

118. Why are you attracted to this belief system?
119. What are the key tenants of this belief system?
120. Why do you feel this belief system is truer than others?
121. If you believe in the concepts of heaven and hell, do you think that there is any salvation outside of your religion?
122. Why do you feel this way?
123. Would you say that you belong to any particular denomination of your religion (such as "Baptist," "Catholic," "Sunni," "Shia," "Orthodox," etc.)?
124. Why do you like this denomination more than others?
125. What are the key tenants of this particular denomination of your religion?
126. Why do you feel this denomination is truer than other denominations?
127. If you believe in the concepts of heaven and hell, do you think that there is any salvation outside of your denomination?
128. Why do you feel this way?
129. How would you define the word "cult"?
130. Do you believe you have an obligation to evangelize your supernatural or spiritual beliefs to other people, to try to convince them?
131. If so, what is your typical method of evangelism?
132. What is your opinion of holy writing? Do you believe there are any divinely inspired texts?
133. If so, which texts do you believe are divinely inspired?
134. If you believe in the divine origin of your scripture, do you think it is infallible (without any errors whatsoever), or do you think human error has crept into this scripture over the years?
135. Can you think of any specific human errors you think have crept into your scripture?
136. Do you believe that the scripture you read, in your part of the world and in your time in history, is complete? Do you believe any divinely inspired writings have been lost from your scripture over the centuries? Do you believe any non-divine

writings have been added to your scripture over the centuries? Do you believe that your scripture is finished, or do you believe that more divinely inspired scriptures may be added to the canon at a later date?

137. Do you believe that all life on Earth was created in six days as described in the book of Genesis, or do you believe that life on Earth evolved gradually over the course of millions of years?

138. If you believe in gradual evolution over millions of years, do you think a divine being guided that evolution, or perhaps set the process in motion, or neither?

139. What do you think children in public schools should be taught, regarding the development of life on Earth? Should children in public schools be taught Darwinian evolution, should they be taught Biblical creationism, should they be taught both, or should they be taught something else entirely?

140. What is your favorite passage from the scriptures?

141. Why does this passage speak to you?

142. What scriptural passage, more than any other, confuses you, or do you wrestle with?

143. Why do you wrestle with that passage?

144. Are you currently a member of any particular church or religious institution?

145. If you are not an official member, are you a regular attendee?

146. If so, which one are you a member or attendee of?

147. Have you ever changed your religious identity (whether changing your entire religion or just changing to a different denomination of the same religion)?

148. If so, why did you do so?

149. Was your change of religious identity a long and gradual process, or did it happen quickly?

150. How did other people around you react when you changed your religious identity?

151. Have you ever changed any specific religious opinions of yours?

152. If so, what prompted you to change those individual opinions?

153. Did you face any backlash from other people for changing those religious opinions?

154. Have you ever faced any mistreatment or persecution for your religious persuasions?

155. If so, what happened?

156. Have you ever wanted to go into the ministry professionally (as a pastor, priest, nun, missionary, evangelist, etc.)?

157. If so, why did you eventually decide for or against going into the ministry?

158. Have you ever had any mystical religious experiences (such as visions, prophetic dreams, tongues-speaking, healings, etc.)?

159. If so, what were they?

160. How convinced are you that this experience was real, on a scale of 1 to 10 (10 being "totally convinced")? Looking back, have you ever had any doubts about it?

161. Do you believe that deceased souls ever come back to this world as ghosts?

162. If so, do you feel that you have ever had an experience with ghosts?

163. If so, what happened?

164. How convinced are you that this experience was real, on a scale of 1 to 10 (10 being "totally convinced")? Looking back, have you ever had any doubts about it?

165. Do you believe in the existence of spirits, angels, and/or demons?

166. If so, do you feel that you have ever had an experience with such spirits?

167. If so, what happened?

168. How convinced are you that this experience was real, on a scale of 1 to 10 (10 being "totally convinced")? Looking back, have you ever had any doubts about it?

169. Do you believe that humans can literally become an angel or a demon, after death?

170. Do you believe that humans can communicate with the souls of the deceased?

171. If so, do you feel that you have ever communicated with the soul of a deceased person or that the soul of a deceased person has ever communicated with you?

172. If so, what happened?

173. How convinced are you that this experience was real, on a scale of 1 to 10 (10 being "totally convinced")? Looking back, have you ever had any doubts about it?

174. Do you believe in the existence of psychic phenomena, like mind-reading, second sight, or the ability to move objects with the mind?

175. Why or why not?

176. Do you believe in astrology? Why or why not? What is your astrological "sign"?

177. How do you believe the world or the universe will ultimately end (speaking as generally, or in as much detail, as you prefer)?

178. What informs your beliefs on the subject of "the end of the world" or "the end of the universe"?

179. Do you believe in the existence of alien life on other planets?

180. Why or why not?

181. If so, do you think scientists will discover basic life forms on other planets within your lifetime?

182. Why or why not?

183. How do you think the discovery of basic life forms on other planets will influence society here on Earth? Will it change our perspective on life, or will it change the way that humans deal with one another?

184. Why do you feel that way?

185. Do you expect to see contact with an intelligent extraterrestrial civilization within your lifetime?

186. Why or why not?

187. How do you think the discovery of an intelligent extraterrestrial civilization will influence society here on Earth? Will it change

our perspective on life, or will it change the way that humans deal with one another?

188. Why do you feel that way?

189. Do you believe that homosexuality is immoral?

190. Why or why not?

191. In your younger years, did people ever talk about homosexuals, or was the issue simply never acknowledged?

192. In your younger years, what would have happened to someone in your community if they had come out openly as a homosexual?

193. Why do you think your community would have reacted that way in your younger years?

194. How do you think your parents would have reacted if one of their children had come out as a homosexual?

195. Why do you think your parents would have reacted that way?

196. Did you ever know any homosexuals or suspected homosexuals?

197. If so, how did you get along with them?

198. Do you think the government should or should not recognize same-sex marriage?

199. Why or why not?

200. Do you think that if children need a home, they should be allowed to be adopted by same-sex couples?

201. Why or why not?

202. Do you think that single, unmarried individuals should be allowed to adopt children?

203. Why or why not?

204. Have you ever had any doubts about your choice of religion?

205. If so, what were those doubts and how did you overcome them?

206. If you believe in the supernatural, what is your opinion on atheists and atheism?

207. Why do you feel that way?

208. In your younger years, did you ever know any people who said they did not believe in any god or anything supernatural whatsoever?

209. If so, did these people profess their lack of belief openly, or did they keep quiet about it?

210. In your younger years, what would have happened to someone in your community if they had claimed to be an atheist?

211. Why do you think your community would have reacted that way?

212. How do you think your parents would have reacted if one of their children had claimed to be an atheist?

213. Why do you think your parents would have reacted that way?

214. Do you think that sometimes catastrophes (such as natural disasters, diseases, financial crashes, or military/terrorist attacks) are ever forms of divine punishment from God?

215. If so, can you think of specific national catastrophes that you believe definitely do constitute divine punishments?

216. If you believe some catastrophes are divine punishments, what specific sins do you feel that those punishments were for?

217. If you were ever in a total vegetative state, would you prefer to have the "plug pulled," or would you prefer to be kept alive in case a cure could be found?

218. Why do you feel this way?

219. What if you were in a partial vegetative state, i.e. you drifted back and forth between being vegetative and partial consciousness? Would you still feel the same way?

220. Why do you feel that way?

221. When was the first time that you really had to come to terms with the concepts of death and mortality? What happened?

222. How had you thought about death and mortality before that instance, and how did you think about it afterward?

223. Have you ever had a close brush with death, or been diagnosed with a terminal illness?

224. If so, what happened?

225. If you've ever been faced with your own mortality, what thoughts and emotions went through your mind at the time?

226. If you've ever been faced with your own mortality, how did your values—what you feel to be important or unimportant—change in that moment?

227. After you pass away, would you prefer to be buried whole or cremated? Why do you feel that way?

228. If you prefer being cremated, what do you want to be done with your ashes?

229. Do you have a burial plot already picked out?

230. Where do you want to be buried, and next to whom?

231. Why would you like to be buried there?

232. Do you intend to donate any of your body to organ donations or to scientific research?

233. Why or why not?

234. What code or list of principles do you live your life by?

235. If you could sum up your spiritual worldview in one word, what would it be?

Previous Generations

1. Who was the oldest relative of yours that you ever met? How old were they?
2. Have you ever seen a "family bible" for your family that contains names, births, anniversaries, and deaths of family members?
3. If so, who owned this family bible?
4. Do you remember seeing any photographs or portraits of your ancestors when you were younger?
5. Do you remember being told who the people in those photographs were?
6. What did the people in those photographs look like? What were they wearing? What were their facial expressions like? Do you remember their hair color, hair style, skin color, or if there holding any object like a cane or umbrella?
7. What is the oldest photograph or portrait that you personally own?
8. Who is in this picture?
9. Where is this picture stored or displayed currently?
10. Were you adopted, or raised by anyone other than your birth parents?
11. If so, do you know who your birth parents were?
12. If you were raised by someone other than your birth parents, how do you feel about the fact that you were raised by someone other than your birth parents?
13. If you were raised by someone other than your birth parents, what would you say to your birth parents right now, if you could?
14. If you were raised by someone other than your birth parents, do you remember how, when, and why you went into the care of your foster, adoptive, or step parent(s)?
15. If so, how did you feel at the time, when you went into the care of your foster, adoptive, or step parent(s)?

16. If you were raised by someone other than your birth parents, what would you say the biggest differences are between your birth parents and your foster, adoptive, or step parent(s)?

17. Do you remember any of your grandparents or great grandparents?

18. Which ones?

19. Were they one of your father's parents, one of your mother's parents, one of your father's grandparents, or one of your mother's grandparents?

20. Do you remember any of your uncles, aunts, great uncles, or great aunts?

21. Which ones?

22. Were they your father's sibling, your mother's sibling, or one of your grandparents' siblings?

For the following questions (#23 - #155), feel free to replace "relative" with "father," "mother," "grandparent," "great grandparent," "uncle/aunt," "great uncle/aunt," or whichever relative you would like to learn more about. It may help to repeat questions #23 - #155 for each older relative that the interviewee met.

23. What did this relative look like? (How tall were they? Were they thin or round? What color was their hair? etc.)

24. Do you remember the sound of this relative's voice? (Was it high or low pitched? Was it smooth or gravely? Was it clear or mumbly? Was it loud or soft? Did they speak quickly or with a drawl? Did they speak with any accent or have any verbal quirks?)

25. Did this relative speak more than one language?

26. If so, which languages?

27. How fluent were they in these languages?

28. How, why, and when did they learn each of these languages?

29. Can you describe this relative's laugh?

30. Can you mimic this relative's voice from memory, right now?
31. Did this relative have any unique little habits or tics?
32. If so, what were they?
33. What did this relative smell like? Did they wear any perfume, cologne, aftershave, etc.? Did their job give them a distinctive scent (for instance, a woodworker smelling like sawdust, a mechanic smelling like engine oil, a cook smelling like a certain food or spice, etc.)?
34. What was this relative's personality like? (Were they warm, extroverted, cool, quiet, generous, frugal, funny, serious, etc.?)
35. Did this relative ever recite any rhymes or sing any songs?
36. If so, what were they?
37. Can you remember the words to those rhymes or songs?
38. Did this relative ever play any musical instruments?
39. If so, which ones?
40. If this relative played musical instruments, can you remember any particular songs they would play on the instruments?
41. If this relative played musical instruments, do you know where the instruments that this relative owned currently exist?
42. What is your very earliest memory of this relative?
43. How did this relative interact with you? How did they treat you?
44. What sort of things did you do together with this relative?
45. How often did you get to see this relative?
46. Did you ever stay or live with this relative for an extended amount of time?
47. If so, what was the reason?
48. If you stayed with this relative, how long did you stay with them?
49. If you stayed with this relative, what did you do during your stay?
50. Where did this relative live?
51. What was the property and neighborhood around this relative's house like?
52. What did this relative's house (both outside and inside) look like?
53. What did this relative's house smell like?
54. What kind of furniture did this relative have in their house?

55. Did this relative have any pets?

56. If so, what kind of animals?

57. If this relative had pets, what were the names of the pets?

58. Do you know who picked the pets' names, and why those names were chosen?

59. Do you know how this relative got these pets?

60. What were the pets like? How did they act?

61. Do you remember when any of these pets died?

62. How did your relative's pet(s) die?

63. How did you feel when this relative's pet(s) died?

64. Who else did this relative live with?

65. If this relative was married, who was their spouse?

66. Did this relative ever tell how they met, dated, and married their spouse?

67. If so, what was the story?

68. Can you describe the relationship dynamic that this relative had with their spouse? How did they interact with their spouse?

69. How did this relative show affection to their spouse?

70. How did this relative fight or argue with their spouse?

71. Do you remember any of this relative's neighbors?

72. If so, can you recall their names?

73. What were these neighbors like?

74. In what way(s) did these neighbors interact with your relative, and with you?

75. Do you remember any of this relative's friends who would come to visit?

76. If so, can you recall their names?

77. What were these friends like?

78. In what way(s) did these friends of your relative interact with your relative, and with you?

79. Did this relative ever give you any gifts?

80. If so, what were they?

81. If this relative gave you any gifts, what was the occasion?

82. How did this relative celebrate holidays like Christmas, Thanksgiving, Easter, birthdays, etc.?
83. Did you ever celebrate any holidays with this relative?
84. What were those celebrations like?
85. Did this relative emigrate from another country?
86. If so, which one?
87. If this relative was an immigrant, did they ever talk about their home country?
88. If so, what kind of stories or facts did they say?
89. If this relative was an immigrant, did they ever talk about their reasons for immigrating?
90. If so, what did they say?
91. What kind of topics did this relative like to chat about?
92. Did this relative ever tell any stories about their childhood?
93. If so, what were they?
94. Do you happen to know if this relative belonged to any particular political party or not?
95. If so, which one?
96. Did this relative ever talk about politics?
97. If so, what opinions did they express?
98. Do you know what religion and denomination this relative belonged to?
99. Do you know if this relative was a member of any particular place of worship?
100. If so, which one was it?
101. How regularly did they attend this place of worship?
102. Did this relative ever talk about religion or their spirituality? If so, what insights did they share?
103. Was this relative a member of any societies or organizations (like a Masonic Lodge, a VFW post, the American Legion Ladies Auxiliary, etc.)? If so, which ones? Did they hold any titles?
104. What is the most valuable thing that you can remember this relative ever owning?

105. Did this relative ever tell stories or facts about their parents or grandparents? If so, what did they say?

106. Do you remember any memorable quotes or sayings that this relative uttered?

107. How did this relative interact with other relatives, such as your parents, grandparents, uncles, aunts, cousins, or siblings?

108. What kinds of foods or drinks do you remember this relative consuming?

109. How large were the meals that they ate?

110. Did this relative like to cook or prepare meals?

111. If so, what did they cook?

112. Did they follow a cookbook, hand-written family recipes, or did they cook from memory?

113. Did you ever inherit any family recipes from this relative?

114. Do you know how this relative had earned a living, during their working years?

115. Did this relative ever say how they got their name (perhaps if they were named after anyone)?

116. Did this relative have any nicknames?

117. If their nickname was not just a shortened version of their full name, did this relative ever mention how they earned their nickname?

118. Did this relative ever talk about witnessing or living through any major historical events, like natural disasters, economic depressions, assassinations, wars, the ends of wars, etc.?

119. When was the happiest that you ever saw this relative?

120. How did this relative act when they were in an especially cheerful mood?

121. When was the saddest that you ever saw this relative?

122. Do you ever remember seeing this relative being particularly afraid of something?

123. Did this relative ever do anything that grossed you out?

124. When was the angriest that you ever saw this relative?

125. When was the most worried that you ever saw this relative?

126. Had this relative ever lost anyone close to them, such as a child or sibling or spouse?
127. If so, did this relative ever speak about how the loss affected them? Did they ever talk about missing this lost loved one, or reminisce about what this lost loved one was like when they were alive?
128. What was this relative's way of showing affection?
129. What did this relative like to do for fun in their spare time?
130. Did this relative have any favorite television or radio shows?
131. How did this relative change as they aged?
132. What kind of health issues did this relative deal with?
133. Did you see this relative in their last days?
134. If so, what were they like?
135. Do you remember the last thing this relative ever said to you?
136. When did this relative die?
137. Where did this relative die?
138. Do you know the cause of this relative's death? If so, what was it?
139. Were you at this relative's side when they died?
140. Do you know if anyone was at this relative's side when they died? If so, whom?
141. Do you happen to know what the last words this relative uttered were?
142. If so, what were they?
143. How did you feel when you found out that this relative had died?
144. Did you attend the funeral of this relative?
145. If so, do you remember where the funeral of this relative took place?
146. Were all of this relative's living immediate family in attendance at the funeral, or was there anyone you remember who couldn't make it?
147. Did you see anyone at this relative's funeral who you were not expecting to see?

148. Do you recall any memorable stories or anecdotes told about this relative in any of the eulogies given at their funeral?

149. What was the weather like on the day of this relative's funeral and burial?

150. Do you know which cemetery this relative is buried in?

151. Do you remember about how far the cemetery was from the funeral location?

152. What did you and your family do immediately after the burial of this relative? Was there any sort of family get-together afterward? Did you go to visit another relative? Did you go straight home?

153. Did you inherit any heirlooms from this relative?

154. If so, what were they?

155. If you inherited any heirlooms from this relative, do you still have them?

156. Did anyone ever tell you the meaning of your last name? What did they say was the meaning?

157. What is your eye color, and who do you think you inherited that from?

158. Has your hair color changed over the years to what it is now?

159. What was your hair color when you were younger, and who do you think you inherited that from?

160. How tall are you, and who do you think you inherited your height or shortness from?

161. Have there ever been five generations alive in your family at the same time? (i.e. someone who was alive at the same time as their great great grandchild?)

162. If so, who was the great great grandchild, and how was that child descended from the living great great grandparent?

163. If there have been five generations in your family alive at the same time, are there any photographs of the great great grandparent and the great great grandchild together, or are there any photographs of all five generations together? If so, do you know who owns that photograph, or where it is?

164. Have there ever been six generations alive in your family at the same time? (i.e. someone who was alive at the same time as their great great great grandchild?)

165. If so, who was the great great great grandchild, and how was that child descended from the living great great great grandparent?

166. If there have been six generations in your family alive at the same time, are there any photographs of the great great great grandparent and the great great great grandchild together, or are there any photographs of all six generations together?

167. If so, do you know who owns that photograph, or where it is?

168. Did you ever hear any interesting stories about ancestors that you never met? Who were the ancestors, and what were the stories?

169. Have you ever attended any family reunions?

170. If so, which family was the reunion or reunions for?

171. Do you remember meeting any memorable or particularly elderly family members at these reunions?

172. What was the biggest family reunion you ever attended?

173. Which branch of the family was your biggest family reunion for?

174. Where and when was your biggest family reunion?

175. About how many family members were at your biggest family reunion?

176. Who can you think of, in your family tree, who lived the longest?

177. What was the most memorable or significant birthday party that you ever attended?

178. What happened at that birthday party?

179. Who do you know, in your family tree, who has celebrated a 50th wedding anniversary?

180. Who do you know, in your family tree, who has celebrated a 60th wedding anniversary?

181. Who do you know, in your family tree, who has celebrated a 70th wedding anniversary?

182. Who can you think of, in your family tree, who was married for the longest amount of time?

183. What is the most memorable wedding anniversary celebration that you ever attended?

184. What happened at that anniversary celebration?

185. Who, amongst the previous generations in your family tree, do you think was the strongest person?

186. What about that person makes you think that?

187. Can you recall any specific memory where you were impressed with their strength?

188. Who, amongst the previous generations in your family tree, do you think was the smartest person?

189. What about that person makes you think that?

190. Can you recall any specific memory where you were impressed with their intelligence?

191. Who, amongst the previous generations in your family tree, do you think was the funniest person?

192. What about that person makes you think that?

193. Can you recall any specific memory where you were impressed with their sense of humor?

194. Who, amongst the previous generations in your family tree, do you think was the kindest person?

195. What about that person makes you think that?

196. Can you recall any specific memory where you were impressed with their kindness?

197. Who, amongst the previous generations in your family tree, do you think was the most inspiring person?

198. What about that person makes you think that?

199. Can you recall any specific memory of them that particularly inspired you?

200. Who, amongst the previous generations in your family tree, did you look up to and try to emulate the most?

201. What about that person makes you think that?

202. Can you recall any specific memory of them that made you want to be like them?

203. Who, amongst the previous generations in your family tree, was the best with children?

204. What about that person makes you think that?

205. Can you recall any specific memory of them that exemplified how good they were with children?

206. Who, amongst the previous generations in your family tree, lived the most adventurous and interesting life?

207. What about that person makes you think that?

208. Can you recall any specific memories of them doing something particularly adventurous or interesting?

209. Who, amongst the previous generations in your family tree, do you think was the most religious or spiritual person?

210. What about that person makes you think that?

211. Can you recall any specific memory of them that exemplified their religiosity or spirituality?

212. Who, amongst the previous generations in your family tree, do you think was the least religious?

213. What about that person makes you think that?

214. Can you recall any specific memory of them that exemplified their non-religiousness?

215. Who, amongst the previous generations in your family tree, do you think was the most giving and generous?

216. What about that person makes you think that?

217. Can you recall any specific memory where you were impressed with their generosity?

218. Who, amongst the previous generations in your family tree, do you think was the best cook?

219. What were their best dishes, and why did you like them so much?

220. Who, amongst the previous generations in your family tree, do you think was the most artistically talented?

221. What about that person makes you think that?

222. Can you recall any specific memory where you were impressed with their artistic ability?

223. Do you personally own any art that this relative created?

224. Where can this relative's art be found?

225. Who, amongst the previous generations in your family tree, do you think was the most musically talented?

226. What about that person makes you think that?

227. Can you recall any specific memory where you were impressed with their musical ability?

228. Do you have any recordings of this relative's music?

229. Where can recordings of this relative's music be found?

230. Who, amongst the previous generations in your family tree, do you think was the most stylish or best-dressed?

231. What about that person makes you think that?

232. Can you recall any specific memory where you were impressed with their stylishness?

233. Which man, amongst the previous generations in your family tree, do you think was the most handsome?

234. What about that person makes you think that?

235. Which woman, amongst the previous generations in your family tree, do you think was the most pretty?

236. What about that person makes you think that?

237. Who, amongst the previous generations in your family tree, did you most enjoy visiting?

238. Why did you enjoy visiting this relative so much?

239. Can you recall a specific memory of a particularly enjoyable visit?

240. Who, amongst the previous generations in your family tree, do you think was the most patient and longsuffering?

241. What about that person makes you think that?

242. Can you recall any specific memory where you were impressed with their patience?

243. Who, amongst the previous generations in your family tree, do you think was the tidiest and cleanest?

244. What about that person makes you think that?

245. Can you recall any specific memory where you were impressed with their tidiness?

246. Who, amongst the previous generations in your family tree, do you think was the messiest?

247. What about that person makes you think that?

248. Can you recall any specific memory where you were impressed with their messiness?

249. Who, amongst the previous generations in your family tree, loved animals the most?

250. What about that person makes you think that?

251. Can you recall any specific memory where you were impressed with their love for animals?

252. Who, amongst the previous generations in your family tree, was the best at doing whatever they tried their hand at?

253. What about that person makes you think that?

254. Can you recall any specific memory where you were impressed with their handiness?

255. Who, amongst the previous generations in your family tree, was the most prone to saying exactly what was on their mind?

256. What about that person makes you think that?

257. Can you recall any specific memory of that relative saying something strikingly honest?

258. Who, amongst the previous generations in your family tree, was the most unprejudiced and accepting of different people from different backgrounds?

259. What about that person makes you think that?

260. Can you recall any specific memory where you were impressed with how accepting and unprejudiced they were?

261. Who, amongst the previous generations in your family tree, was the most hard-working?

262. What about that person makes you think that?

263. Can you recall any specific memory where you were impressed with how hard-working they were?

264. Who in your family worked until the oldest age before retiring?

265. What work did they do in their later years, how old where they when they stopped working?

266. Why did this relative eventually stop working?

267. Who, amongst the previous generations in your family tree, was the most social and active in their community?

268. What about that person makes you think that?

269. Can you recall any specific memory where you were impressed with their social activity?

270. Who, amongst the previous generations in your family tree, kept to themselves the most?

271. What about that person makes you think that?

272. Can you recall any specific memory where you were impressed with their solitude?

273. Who, amongst the previous generations in your family tree, do you think was the most talkative and chatty?

274. What kind of subjects would this relative talk about?

275. Who, amongst the previous generations in your family tree, do you think was the quietest?

276. How quiet was this relative?

277. Was there a reason this relative was so quiet?

278. Who, amongst the previous generations in your family tree, was the largest/tallest in size?

279. About how big were they?

280. Who, amongst the previous generations in your family tree, was the shortest or most petite?

281. About how small were they?

282. Who, amongst the previous generations in your family tree, lived the farthest away from the rest of the family?

283. Where did this relative live?

284. Who, amongst the previous generations in your family tree, lived in the biggest house?

285. How big was this house, and where was it located?

286. Who, amongst the previous generations in your family tree, lived in the nicest house?

287. Where was this house located, and why did you think this house was so nice?

288. Who, amongst the previous generations in your family tree, lived in the smallest house?

289. How small was this house, and where was it located?

290. Which branch of the family can you remember that inhabited the same house for the longest number of years?

291. Where was this house, and how long did this house stay in the family?

292. Who was the wealthiest or most successful person in your family tree?

293. How did they earn their wealth?

294. What did you call each of your grandparents?

295. Can you think of people in your family tree who had nicknames unrelated to their real names? (i.e., a person named Fred being

nicknamed "Buck," or a person named Hilda being nicknamed "Sparky", etc.)

296. How and why did those people get those nicknames?

297. Did anyone ever tell you which countries your ancestors came from?

298. If so, can you remember, by name, specific ancestors who came from specific countries?

299. Do you take pride in being descended from a certain ethnicity or having ancestry from a certain country?

300. How proud are you of having that ancestry?

301. Why do you take pride in being of that ethnicity or having ancestry from a certain country?

302. Do you remember hearing any family legends about stowaways or illegal immigrants?

303. If so, which ancestors were said to be stowaways or illegal immigrants?

304. Did you ever hear about any Native American blood in the family?

305. Did you ever hear about any royal blood in the family?

306. Did you ever hear stories about being related to any famous individuals?

307. Did you ever hear stories about being related to any infamous individuals?

308. Did you ever hear about any of your ancestors suffering persecution or mistreatment on account of their ethnicity or skin color?

309. Did you ever hear about any of your ancestors suffering persecution or mistreatment on account of their religious beliefs?

310. Did you ever hear about any of your ancestors suffering persecution or mistreatment on account of their political beliefs?

311. What are some skills that your parents or grandparents possessed that you wish they could have taught you, but they never were able to?

312. Can you remember a time when one of your grandparents surprised you with their physical strength or their wisdom?

313. If you could bring one deceased relative back to life, who would you choose?

314. If you could bring one deceased relative back to life, what would you ask them?

315. Which of your ancestors do you think you are most similar to in personality?

316. Why do you feel that way?

317. Which of your ancestors do you think you are most similar to in appearance?

318. Why do you think so?

319. Which of your ancestors did you have the closest bond with?

320. Why did you have such a close bond with them?

321. If you had to sum up your family tree in just one word, what would it be?

World Events

1. Did you ever see or meet any presidents, presidential candidates, war generals, etc.?
2. Did you have any communication with them?
3. If so, what did you say to one another?
4. Did any of your older relatives ever talk about seeing or meeting any presidents, presidential candidates, war generals, etc.?
5. Did they ever have any communication with them?
6. If so, what did they say to one another?
7. Did you ever meet or see any old U.S. Civil War veterans in your younger years?
8. If so, had they been a Union or a Confederate soldier?
9. If you met a U.S. Civil War veteran, what did they say to you?
10. What is your opinion on the issue of displaying the Confederate flag?
11. Did your parents or grandparents ever talk about World War 1?
12. If so, how did they say that World War 1 affected their lives?
13. Did you ever know anyone who served in the military during World War 1?
14. If so, did they ever share any stories about their time in the military during World War 1?
15. If so, what were the stories?
16. Did your parents or grandparents ever talk about Prohibition?
17. If so, how did they say that Prohibition affected their lives?
18. Did your parents or grandparents ever tell any stories about the Prohibition era?

19. Were you alive during the Great Depression?
20. Do you remember the Black Tuesday stock market crash on October 29th, 1929?
21. If so, do you recall how your family reacted on Black Tuesday?
22. How did the Great Depression affect your family?
23. What kind of meals did your family eat during the Great Depression?
24. Do you remember going hungry often, during that era?
25. Where did your family's food usually come from, during the Great Depression?
26. How would you help to provide for the family, during the Great Depression?
27. What kind of sacrifices did your family have to make, during the Great Depression?
28. How did your family earn money during the Great Depression?
29. Was anyone in your family unable to find employment during the Great Depression?
30. Did anyone in your family lose their job during the Great Depression?
31. Did the bad state of the economy have an effect upon the cheerfulness or optimism in your family's home?
32. Did anyone in your family ever lose hope for the future during the Great Depression, or did everyone always believe that things would eventually get better?
33. Did you see any families suffering worse than yours, during the Great Depression?
34. If so, what were these other families' plights like?
35. What is the number one lesson or piece of wisdom that you learned from the Great Depression?
36. If you had to sum up your experience during the Great Depression in one word, what would it be?

37. Were you alive during World War 2?

38. Do you remember the Spanish Civil War and the Japanese invasion of China in the run-up to World War 2 in the late 1930s?

39. If so, did you or anyone you know anticipate that the Spanish Civil War and the Japan-China War would pave the way for a bigger war that would involve your country, or did people assume that it was just small foreign wars?

40. Do you remember when Germany invaded Poland on September 1st, 1939?

41. Was there any feeling in your household that this might lead to a larger war that would involve your country?

42. (If the interviewee is American) Since America was neutral at this early point, did people in your household or community tend to side with Germany before America entered the war, or did they side with Poland and Britain and France before America entered the war?

43. (If the interviewee is American) Before America took a side in World War 2, many German-Americans were sympathetic to Germany, and some even went to Germany to fight for their fatherland. Did you ever hear or know of any German-Americans going to Germany to join the German military before 1941?

44. Did your family ever receive any letters from any cousins or relatives who lived in one of the enemy countries? If so, what kinds of things were said in the correspondence?

45. Before the bombing of Pearl Harbor, do you remember anyone saying that they thought America should enter the war? What reasons did they give?

46. Before the bombing of Pearl Harbor, do you remember anyone saying that they thought America should stay out of the war? What reasons did they give?

47. Do you remember the bombing of Pearl Harbor on December 7th, 1941?

48. Where were you when you heard the news of the attack on Pearl Harbor?

49. How did you first find out that it had happened?

50. How did you react when you heard the news?

51. How did the members of your family react when they heard the news?

52. How did your community react?

53. Do you remember what the weather was like where you lived, on the day of the bombing of Pearl Harbor?

54. Do you remember anyone still advocating for America to stay out of the war, even after the attack on Pearl Harbor?

55. Do you remember when Germany and Italy declared war on the United States a few days after Pearl Harbor?

56. What was your reaction, and what emotions did you feel, when Germany and Italy declared war on the United States?

57. Do you recall any backlash or anger against Germans, Italians, or Asians living in your community?

58. How did you feel after President Roosevelt in turn declared war on the Axis Powers in December of 1941?

59. How much social pressure was there on young men in your community to join the military? Was it expected of the men? Did women shame the men who hadn't joined the military yet?

60. How do you feel that your country's entry into World War 2 affected the state of the economy? Did it make the Great Depression better or worse?

61. Do you remember your family or community losing any young men during the war?

62. If so, how did you react upon learning of the young man's death?

63. How did your family react to the young man's death?

64. How did your community react to the young man's death?

65. How did you feel about the state of the world, during World War 2?

66. Did you ever really fear that Hitler or the Japanese Empire would actually conquer your country, or did you always rest assured that your country would be victorious?

67. How did your country's entry into World War 2 change your everyday life?

68. Did you ever have bomb drills in school to practice in case Axis warplanes bombed your neighborhood?

69. Do you remember seeing any war-related posters hanging around your town, denouncing the Axis powers and urging men to join the military?

70. What did these posters look like, and what did they say?

71. Did you have any close friends or family members serving in the military during World War 2?

72. If so, how did you feel when they were deployed? Did you fear for their safety?

73. What kind of letters did you receive from your friends or family members who were serving in the war?

74. Did you ever send any letters to them?

75. If so, what did you say?

76. Did any of your friends or family members who were serving in the war ever come home temporarily on furlough?

77. If so, did you spend time with them while they were home?

78. How did they spend their furlough? What kind of things did they do while they were visiting home?

79. When your friends or family members were home from the war on furlough, did they ever express anxiety about having to go back to war?

80. Did you ever hear about any special acts of heroism by any of your friends or family members who were serving in the war?

81. If so, who was it, and what were the heroic acts?

82. Do you remember if your friends or family members who were serving in the war were awarded any medals?

83. Did you ever see any warplanes, tanks, ships, submarines, or squadrons of soldiers near your community, during the course of the war?

84. What responsibilities were put on women in your community during the war?

85. Were you ever imprisoned or interned by enemy forces? If so, what happened?

86. Were you ever put into an internment camp by your own government, during the war? If so, what happened?

87. Do you remember when President Franklin Roosevelt died on April 12th, 1945?

88. How did you react when you heard the news of Roosevelt's death?

89. What emotions did you feel when you heard the news?

90. How did other people in your family react when they heard the news of Roosevelt's death?

91. How did your community react to Roosevelt's death?

92. Do you remember what the weather was like in your area, on the day of Roosevelt's death?

93. What had been you and your family's opinions of Franklin Roosevelt before his death?

94. What were you and your family's opinions of Franklin Roosevelt after his death?

95. Do you remember seeing pictures or recordings of Franklin Roosevelt's funeral? What do you remember about it?

96. What were your family's opinions of and expectations for Harry Truman when he became president, following FDR's death?

97. Do you recall when you heard the news of the atomic bombing of Hiroshima and Nagasaki in August of 1945?

98. What was your reaction to the news that atomic bombs had been used in Japan?

99. Do you remember what kinds of things people in your community were saying about the fact that atomic bombs had been used in Japan?

100. Do you think most people's opinion of Harry Truman's presidency has changed between the time he was president and today? How so?

101. When did you first hear that the war had ended in August of 1945?

102. How did you react when you heard the news that the war was over?

103. How did members of your family react to the news that the war was over?

104. How did your community react to the news that the war was over?

105. Do you remember when your friends or family members who had been serving in World War 2 finally came home?

106. How did you and your family greet them when they came home?

107. What did they do or say when they finally arrived home?

108. Were any celebrations held in your community after the end of the war?

109. Immediately after World War 2 had ended, do you recall there being any fear that the peace might not last, and war might soon break out again?

110. What is the number one lesson or piece of wisdom that you learned from World War 2?

111. If you had to sum up your experience living through World War 2 in one word, what it would be?

112. Were you alive during the Cuban Missile Crisis in October of 1962?

113. What did you think about the crisis while it was happening?

114. How did your family react to the crisis?

115. Did people actually believe that nuclear war was imminent?

116. Were you alive when President John F. Kennedy was assassinated on November 22nd, 1963?

117. Do you remember where you were when you heard the news?

118. How did you hear the news of JFK's assassination?

119. How did you react when you heard the news?

120. Do you remember what the weather was like on the day of JFK's assassination?

121. How did your family members react when they heard the news?

122. How did your community react after hearing the news?

123. What did you do the rest of the day after the assassination?

124. What did you do the next day after the assassination?

125. What did you feel like in the days after the assassination?

126. Had your family been admirers of JFK before the assassination?

127. What did people in your household think of JFK after the assassination?

128. Do you remember seeing pictures or video of JFK's funeral? What do you remember about it?

129. How did you react when you heard that JFK's assassin, Lee Harvey Oswald, had been shot on November 24th, 1963?

130. If you had to sum up John F. Kennedy's presidency in one word, what would it be?

131. Do you remember when Martin Luther King, Jr. was assassinated on April 4th, 1968?

132. What was your reaction to Dr. King's assassination?

133. What emotions did you feel when you learned of Dr. King's assassination?

134. What was your family's reaction to Dr. King's assassination?

135. What was your community's reaction to Dr. King's assassination?

136. Had you or anyone in your family been involved in the Civil Rights Movement of the 1960s?

137. If so, what activities did you take part in, and what are your most poignant memories from the Civil Rights Movement era?

138. Did you ever see much racism in your home town? If so, are there any particular instances of racism you saw that stick out in your memory?

139. Did your parents ever express any opinions on people of other races?

140. Did your grandparents ever express any opinions on people of other races?

141. What had been you and your family's opinions of the Civil Rights movement before Dr. King's assassination?

142. What had been you and your family's opinions of the Civil Rights movement after Dr. King's assassination?

143. What had been you and your family's opinions of Martin Luther King, Jr., personally, before his assassination?

144. What had been you and your family's opinions of Martin Luther King, Jr., personally, after his assassination?

145. Were you alive when Apollo 11 landed on the moon, on July 20th, 1969?

146. Had there been any fear, during Apollo 11's journey, that it might not make it to the moon?

147. Before the Apollo 11 landing, did you ever hear anyone say they thought there might be alien life on the moon?

148. Where were you when you saw the broadcast of the Apollo 11 moon landing?

149. What did you feel when you saw the broadcast of the Apollo 11 moon landing?

150. How did other people in your household react upon seeing the broadcast?

151. Was there any fear, after Apollo 11's landing on the moon, that they might not be able to make it safely back to Earth?

152. Do you remember seeing the picture of the planet Earth rising over the Moon's horizon?

153. If so, did that picture change your perspective on the world at all?

154. Do you remember when the Watergate scandal occurred?

155. What had been you and your family's opinions of President Richard Nixon before Watergate?

156. What had been you and your family's opinions of President Richard Nixon during Watergate?

157. What had been you and your family's opinions of President Richard Nixon after it became clear that Nixon was guilty?

158. Did you ever support impeaching Nixon? Why or why not?

159. Had you been expecting Richard Nixon to be impeached, or did you think it would never actually happen?

160. How did you react when you heard the news that Richard Nixon had resigned from the presidency on August 9th, 1974?

161. What emotions did you feel when you heard that Nixon had resigned?

162. What was your family's reaction to Nixon's resignation?

163. Did anybody in your community express any opinions on Nixon's resignation when it happened?

164. How did you feel about President Gerald Ford's decision to pardon Nixon on September 8th, 1974?

165. What was your family's opinion on Gerald Ford's pardoning of Nixon?

166. Did anybody in your community express any opinions on Ford's pardoning of Nixon when it happened?

167. Did you support or oppose the Vietnam War? Why or why not?

168. Did your family members support or oppose the Vietnam War? Why or why not?

169. Did people in your community generally support or oppose the Vietnam War? Why or why not?

170. Did any of your friends or family members serve in the military in the Vietnam War? If so, whom?

171. How did the Vietnam War affect your friends and family members who served there?

172. What opinions were expressed regarding the war, by the Vietnam War veterans that you personally knew?

173. Do you believe that the American military pulled out of Vietnam too soon, and should have stayed there longer?

174. How did you feel when American involvement in the Vietnam War finally came to an end?

175. Did you support or oppose the Persian Gulf War when it happened in 1990 and 1991? Why or why not?

176. Did you support or oppose the impeachment of President Bill Clinton in 1998? Why or why not?

177. What is your opinion on how First Lady Hillary Clinton handled the Monica Lewinsky scandal in 1998?

178. Do you remember where you were when you heard the news that terrorists had begun attacking the United States on September 11th, 2001?

179. How did you first hear the news of the 9/11 attacks?

180. What was your reaction upon hearing the news? What emotions did you feel as the report of more and more attacks came in?

181. What was your reaction when you heard that the Twin Towers at the World Trade Center had collapsed?

182. Do you remember what the weather was like on that day?

183. Did you ever feel that you were in any personal danger on 9/11?

184. How did the 9/11 attacks that morning change your schedule for the rest of the day?

185. What did you feel on September 12th, the day after the 9/11 attacks?

186. How did you feel when it was announced that the American military would be going to war in Afghanistan?

187. In the run-up to the Iraq War, did you believe that Saddam Hussein was a threat to America's national security, and did you support the idea of invading Iraq to topple Saddam's regime?

188. How did you feel when the American invasion of Iraq began?

189. Did your opinion on the Iraq War change at all, as the war progressed over the years?

190. Did your opinion on the War in Afghanistan change at all, as the war progressed over the years?

191. How did you feel when you heard that Osama bin Laden had been killed?

192. If you were alive at the time, what was your opinion on President Herbert Hoover while he was in office?

193. What is your opinion on President Herbert Hoover now?

194. If you were alive at the time, what was your opinion on President Franklin D. Roosevelt while he was in office?

195. What is your opinion of President Franklin D. Roosevelt now?

196. If you were alive at the time, what was your opinion on President Harry Truman while he was in office?

197. What is your opinion of President Harry Truman now?

198. If you were alive at the time, what was your opinion on President Dwight Eisenhower while he was in office?

199. What is your opinion of President Dwight Eisenhower now?

200. If you were alive at the time, what was your opinion on President John F. Kennedy while he was in office?

201. What is your opinion of President John F. Kennedy now?

202. If you were alive at the time, what was your opinion on President Lyndon B. Johnson while he was in office?

203. What is your opinion of President Lyndon B. Johnson now?

204. If you were alive at the time, what was your opinion on President Richard Nixon while he was in office?

205. What is your opinion of President Richard Nixon now?

206. If you were alive at the time, what was your opinion on President Gerald Ford while he was in office?

207. What is your opinion of President Gerald Ford now?

208. If you were alive at the time, what was your opinion on President Jimmy Carter while he was in office?

209. What is your opinion of President Jimmy Carter now?

210. What was your opinion on President Ronald Reagan while he was in office?

211. What is your opinion of President Ronald Reagan now?

212. What was your opinion on President George H. W. Bush while he was in office?

213. What is your opinion of President George H. W. Bush now?

214. What was your opinion on President Bill Clinton while he was in office?

215. What is your opinion on President Bill Clinton now?

216. What was your opinion on President George W. Bush while he was in office?

217. What is your opinion on President George W. Bush now?

218. How did you feel when America elected the first black U.S. president in 2008?

219. What was your opinion on President Barack Obama early on in his presidency?

220. What is your opinion on President Barack Obama now?

221. What surprised you the most about the most recent presidential election season?

222. Do you remember if there was any major event that happened, on the day that you graduated from high school?

223. Do you remember if there was any major event that happened, on the day that you got engaged?

224. Do you remember if there was any major event that happened, on the day that you were married?

225. Do you remember if there was any major event that happened, on the day that any of your children were born?

226. Do you ever use computers?

227. If not, do you have any desire to learn how to use computers?

228. What happened, the first time you ever tried to use a computer?

229. What is your opinion of the Internet?

230. Do you ever use the Internet?

231. If so, do you have a Facebook account?

232. If you don't use the Internet, do you have any desire to learn how to use the Internet?

233. Do you ever use a cellphone? If so, what kind?

234. If you could go into the past, and bring your childhood self into the here-and-now, what would your childhood self be most surprised to see?

235. What are the biggest ways in which the world has changed, from the time you were a child to the present day?

236. What are the most surprising ways that the world has stayed the same, over your lifetime?

237. When you were a child, did you think that the world would look different than it actually does today? How so?

238. How do you think your country will look in another hundred years?

239. How do you think the world will look in another hundred years?

240. What kind of new technology and inventions do you think we will have a hundred years from now?

241. Do you think that advancing technology has made us better or worse off?

242. If you had to guess, where do you think the next major war will be?

243. Currently, which country's government do you think is the biggest enemy of your country's government?

244. Currently, which country's government do you think is the greatest ally of your country's government?

245. Do you think there will ever be another world war? Why or why not?

246. Have you ever felt like the world was about to end? When and why did you feel this way?

247. If you had to sum up the current state of the world in one word, what would it be?

Your Descendants

1. How many children have you had?
2. What are their full names?
3. How did you decide on the first and middle names for each of your children?
4. Did you ever have a name planned in case the baby turned out to be a different gender than the one that they turned out to be? If so, what was the alternate name for the other gender?
5. Before you had children, did you ever debate about whether you wanted children at all?
6. Do you remember where you were when you found out that you or your spouse was pregnant with each child?
7. How did you feel, each time you found out?
8. How was the news of each pregnancy told to the husband, each time?
9. Were any of the pregnancies a surprise?
10. If you had more than one child, how did your older children react when you told them that there was a new baby on the way?
11. How did your parents react when they found out about the first pregnancy?
12. How did your parents react when they found out about the last pregnancy?
13. Did your parents ever disagree with your choice on naming one of your children?
14. If so, why did they disagree, and what was their suggestion for naming that child?
15. Did your parents, grandparents, or older relatives ever give you any advice on pregnancy and parenting? If so, what was the advice?
16. With each of your children, where were you when it became clear that you or the mother was going into labor? Do you remember what you were doing, each time you realized that the

birth was imminent? Do you remember what was said? How did you get to the hospital?

17. How did you feel after the birth of your first child?

18. How difficult or easy were the births of each of your children?

19. Was anything memorable or funny said after the births of any of your children?

20. Were there ever any miscarriages or stillbirths? If so, in what year(s) did the miscarriage(s) or stillbirth(s) occur?

21. Which aspects of becoming a parent proved to be different than how you had expected parenting to be?

22. What has been the most difficult part of being a parent?

23. What has been the happiest moment of being a parent?

24. What has been the scariest moment of being a parent?

25. What has been the saddest moment of being a parent?

26. What would you say is the best way to encourage a child?

27. What would you say is the best way to discipline a child?

28. Can you remember a time when you stood up for one of your children against someone else who was mistreating them?

29. What was the funniest thing one of your children ever said?

30. What was the funniest thing one of your children ever did?

31. What has been the most embarrassing moment of being a parent?

32. What is the one thing in your time as a spouse and parent that you are most thankful for?

33. If you could rewind time, would you do anything differently, or make any different decisions, as a spouse and/or a parent?

34. What do you consider to be your greatest accomplishment as a spouse and parent?

35. What advice did you give to each of your children before they got married? If none of your children have married, then what advice would you give to your child before they get married?

36. What advice did you give to each of your children when they told you that they were going to have a baby of their own? If you do not have any grandchildren yet, then what advice would

you give to one of your children who was thinking about having a child of their own?

37. What advice would you give to a child or grandchild who wanted to marry someone of a vastly different religion?

38. What advice would you give to a child or grandchild who was having marital troubles with their spouse?

39. What advice would you give to a child or grandchild whose spouse was cheating on them?

40. If you knew that your child or grandchild's spouse was lying to them, would you tell your child or grandchild, or would you leave it to those two to sort out on their own?

41. What advice would you give to a child or grandchild who was butting heads with a boss or coworker at their job?

42. If your child or grandchild was an employer, and if they had an employee who was a bad worker but whose family really needed the money, what advice would you give to your child or grandchild? Would you advise them to fire the bad worker, to keep employing the bad worker for the worker's family's sake, or would you advise something else entirely?

43. What advice would you give to a child or grandchild who was having trouble controlling their own child?

44. What advice would you give to a child or grandchild who kept trying to have a baby, but was unable to?

45. What advice would you give to a child or grandchild who was severely depressed?

46. What advice would you give to a child or grandchild who had just lost a job?

47. What advice would you give to a child or grandchild who just didn't feel like working or having a job?

48. What advice would you give to a child or grandchild who was homeless? Would you take them back into your home for a while, or would you urge them to pick themselves back up?

49. What advice would you give to a child or grandchild who had gotten arrested for a crime?

50. What advice would you give to a child or grandchild who happened to strike it rich?

51. What advice would you give to a child or grandchild who was starting their own business?

52. What advice would you give to a child or grandchild who was running for political office?

53. If your child or grandchild became an elected official, but then became embroiled in a major scandal, would you urge them to resign or would you let them sort it out for themselves?

54. What advice would you give to a child or grandchild who wanted to go live permanently in a foreign country?

55. Do you know the names of all of your grandchildren and/or great grandchildren, if you have any?

56. Do you know if there are any stories behind why the names of your grandchildren and/or great grandchildren were chosen?

57. How did you feel when you held your first grandchild?

58. How did you feel when you held your first great grandchild?

59. What was the funniest thing one of your grandchildren ever said?

60. What medical conditions have you personally dealt with (that you think your descendants should be aware of, in case they inherited them)?

61. What medical conditions are prevalent in your family (that you think your descendants should be aware of, in case they inherited them)?

62. Who do you think you inherited those medical conditions from?

63. What allergies do you have?

64. Did you have any allergies when you were young that you grew out of?

65. If so, what were those allergies, and how long did it take you to grow out of them?

66. Who do you think you inherited those allergies from?

67. What is the most important physical family heirloom that you hope your descendants will preserve and not throw away?

68. What are some non-physical things that you feel like you passed down to all of your descendants?

69. What mistake did you make that you would urge all of your descendants to avoid making?

70. What is something that you feel like you did correctly, that you would urge your descendants to do the same?

71. As you have gotten older, how have your values—what you consider to be important—changed?

72. Do you feel like your life, so far, has gone by slowly or quickly?

73. Looking back, what is one thing that you are very glad that you did?

74. What is one important piece of wisdom that you have learned in just the last five years?

75. What things did you learn in your youth that you feel like young people today never learned?

76. If you could engrave any epitaph on your tombstone that you wanted, what would it be?

77. What is the most important tradition in your family? Why?

78. What is your number one hope for your descendants?

79. What is one thing about the world that you hope will still be the same in 100 years?

80. Do you see any recognizable family traits in me? Like what?

81. What is the one thing you most want future generations to remember about you?

82. If you could give a message to your great grandchildren 100 years from now, what would you say?

About Josiah Schmidt

Josiah Schmidt is a professional genealogist based in Emmetsburg, Iowa. He has been researching genealogy for over a decade, and started a family history research business in 2013. Josiah Schmidt has conducted hundreds of family history interviews with dozens of individuals. Before his career in genealogy, Josiah worked as a campaign consultant, political blogger, and freelance politics writer. As a political journalist, Josiah interviewed dozens of candidates and officials, including three U.S. presidential candidates. Josiah now uses his research, writing, and interviewing skills to help others discover their ancestral stories.

Josiah Schmidt offers his genealogical research services and family history interviewing services for hire, on an hourly commission basis. Josiah specializes in researching Midwestern and German immigrant ancestry, and is able to read, transcribe, and translate old German and English script and handwriting in historical documents. Josiah also offers a service that takes a family's history and turns it into beautifully-illustrated, custom-made children's books that can be enjoyed by generation after generation.

Contact Josiah at: www.SchmidtGen.com.